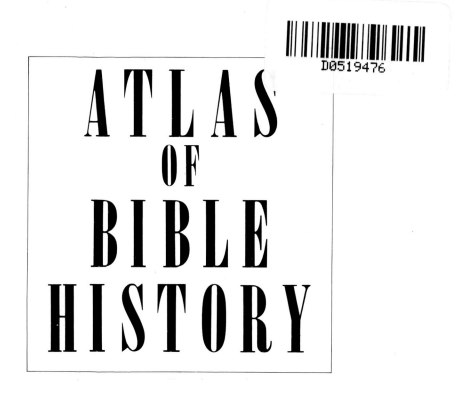

ATLAS
OF
BIBLE
HISTORY

A LION BOOK

Oxford . Batavia . Sydney

Copyright © 1978 and 1986 Lion Publishing

Published by
Lion Publishing plc
Sandy Lane West, Littlemore,
Oxford, England
ISBN 0 7459 1626 0
Lion Publishing Corporation
1705 Hubbard Avenue, Batavia,
Illinois 60510, USA
ISBN 0 7459 1626 0
Albatross Books Pty Ltd
PO Box 320, Sutherland,
NSW 2232, Australia
ISBN 0 7324 0043 0

This new edition, combining
Sections 10 and 12 of
The Lion Encyclopedia of the Bible,
Revised Edition,
first published 1989

Acknowledgements for photographs
British Museum: p.4 (top right)
Tony Deane: pp.4 (three photographs),
  5 (left)
Sonia Halliday Photographs/
  Sonia Halliday: pp.33 (top),39,46,61
  /Jane Taylor: pp.9 (top right and
  bottom),11,27,30
Middle East Photographic Archive: p.10
NASA: p.9 (top)
Picturepoint: pp.5 (bottom),57
Jean-Luc Ray: p.25
All others Lion Publishing/D.S. Alexander

Printed by Zrinski, in Yugoslavia

Contents

Part One
ATLAS OF BIBLE HISTORY

Beginnings: Creation to the Flood and After 4

The World of the Old Testament 6

The Patriarchs: Abraham to Joseph 8

From Egypt to the Promised Land 10

Joshua, the Conquest and the Judges 12

Israel's First Kings: Saul, David and Solomon 14

The Two Kingdoms 16

The Rise of Assyria 18

The Babylonian Invasion 20

The Exile 22

The Return to Jerusalem 24

The Greek Empire and Culture 26

Rome – and the World of the New Testament 28

The Jewish Hope 30

In the Steps of Jesus 32

Pentecost and After: the Spread of the Church 34

Paul's Journeys 36

Part Two
PLACES OF THE BIBLE

A–Z guide of Bible places – from Abana to Zorah 40–64

Map: Israel in the Old Testament 49

Map: Israel in the New Testament 55

Atlas of Bible History

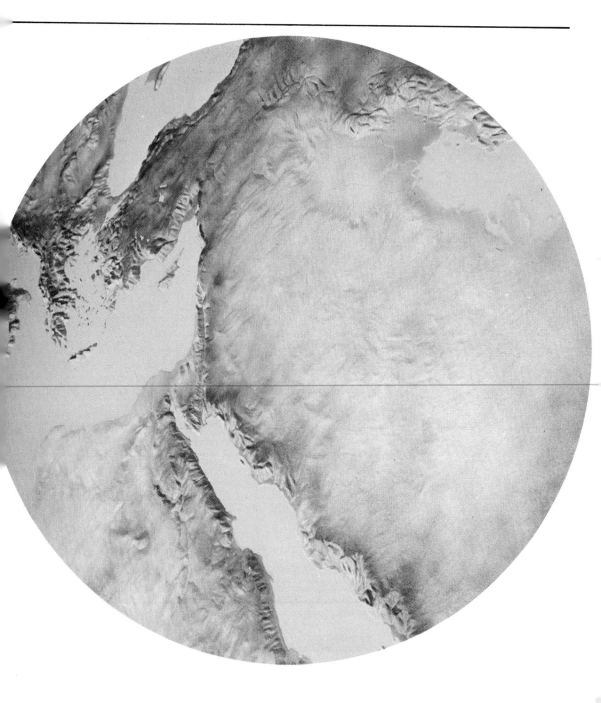

Beginnings: Creation to the Flood and After

The first eleven chapters of Genesis, the first book of the Bible, look back to the very beginning. Our world and everything in it – sun, moon, land and water, birds, animals and every living creature – was made by God. Everything God made was good. And the high point of God's creation was the making of people to take charge of the world and to enjoy God's friendship.

Sadly this perfect world was soon shattered. The first humans, prompted by evil, chose to disobey God. Sin, suffering and death became a permanent part of the pattern of life. The free and open relationship with God was a thing of the past. Already a new creation was needed.

The scene grew darker as evil actions multiplied, until God's judgement became inevitable. The flood was his response. But God had not entirely given up on his world: one good man, Noah, and his family, together with a pair of each bird, animal and reptile, was saved.

God gave Noah the plan for a gigantic boat (the ark) which would float on the rising waters. The measurements given are enormous: about $450 \times 76 \times 45$ ft/$137 \times 23 \times 14$ m (more than half the length of a modern Atlantic liner). It had a wooden framework bound with reeds and sealed with a thick layer of tar.

For five months the rain fell and the flood rose to cover the

The eleventh tablet of the Assyria version of the Epic of Gilgamesh, *which tells the Babylonian story of the flood (seventh century BC).*

earth. It took a further seven and a half months before the ground dried and Noah and h family were able to leave.

God promised that while seed-time and harvest last he will never again destroy the earth by flood: the rainbow is the lasting sign of a promise h will never break.

□ Setting

The story of mankind begins in Eden, placed somewhere in Mesopotamia, the region which became (with Egypt) o: of the two great centres of civilization in the Near East before 3000 BC. The story of Noah, too, belongs here, in t land of the two great rivers,

In the beginning, the Bible says, God created everything that exis – and it was good.

Mt Ararat, in eastern Turkey. The Bible says that Noah's ark grounded on the Ararat range of mountains after the great flood.

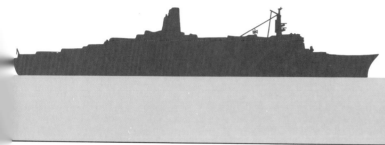

The ark was built to float, on the lines of a barge. It was huge – about half the length of an Atlantic liner – approximately 450ft/137 metres×45ft/14 metres.

Tigris and Euphrates (modern Iran). The ark came to rest, the Bible says, among the mountains of Ararat (in what is now eastern Turkey).

□ **Other stories**
There are other stories besides the Bible account of both the creation and the great flood. Of special interest are the Assyrian and Babylonian stories, also set against a Mesopotamian background.

The World of the Old Testament

The story of ancient Israel, the major theme of the Old Testament begins around 2000 BC. Genesis 11 to the end tells the stories of the Patriarchs, Abraham to Joseph, fathers of the nation, called to be God's people in a special sense.

In the Book of Exodus, God rescues his people from slavery in Egypt, under the leadership of Moses. He gives them his laws at Mt Sinai and establishes the pattern of worship, focussed on the tabernacle – his special tent.

The people's disobedience leads to forty years of camping in the desert before God fulfils his promise to lead them into a new land of their own.

The Book of Joshua describes the conquest of the land and its division amongst the family-clans of Israel.

Judges records a low-point of national life: disobedience to God, invasions, and the heroes

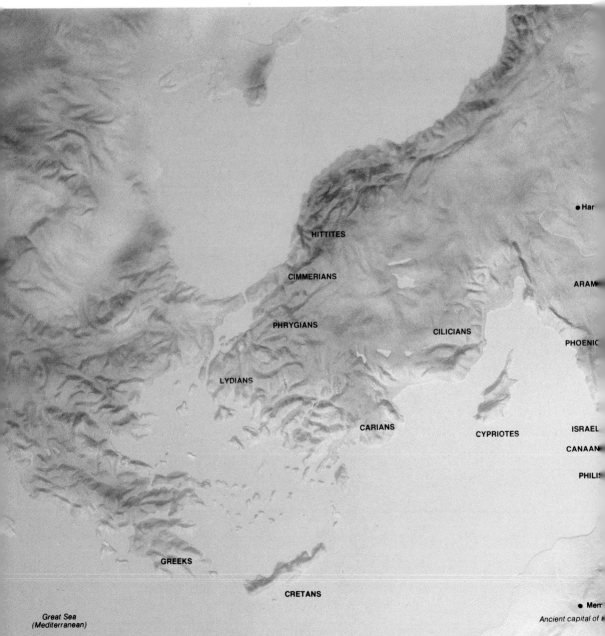

HITTITES

CIMMERIANS

PHRYGIANS

CILICIANS

● Har

ARAM

PHOENIC

LYDIANS

CARIANS

CYPRIOTES

ISRAEL

CANAAN

PHILIS

GREEKS

CRETANS

● Mem

Great Sea
(Mediterranean)

Ancient capital of

EGYPTIANS

God sent to the rescue.

The prophet Samuel heralds the beginning of the monarchy – Israel's first kings, Saul, David and Solomon. The golden age of Solomon, when the temple was built in Jerusalem, ends and the nation splits in two: ten northern breakaway tribes form Israel and two southern tribes with Jerusalem as their capital form Judah.

Great powers rise to the north: Assyria in the ninth century BC and Babylon a century later. Greedy for empire, they swallow up the smaller nations. Israel falls to Assyria, Judah to Babylon – her people taken into exile. God has brought judgement on his people for their constant disobedience and failure to listen to his message through the prophets.

Persia conquers Babylon and the exiled Jews return to rebuild Jerusalem and its temple and re-establish God's worship. Here the Old Testament narrative ends, with the books of Ezra, Nehemiah and Esther.

The events in this 1,500-year saga are played out against the background of a world centred on the eastern Mediterranean, stretching south to include Egypt and east through Persia (Iran).

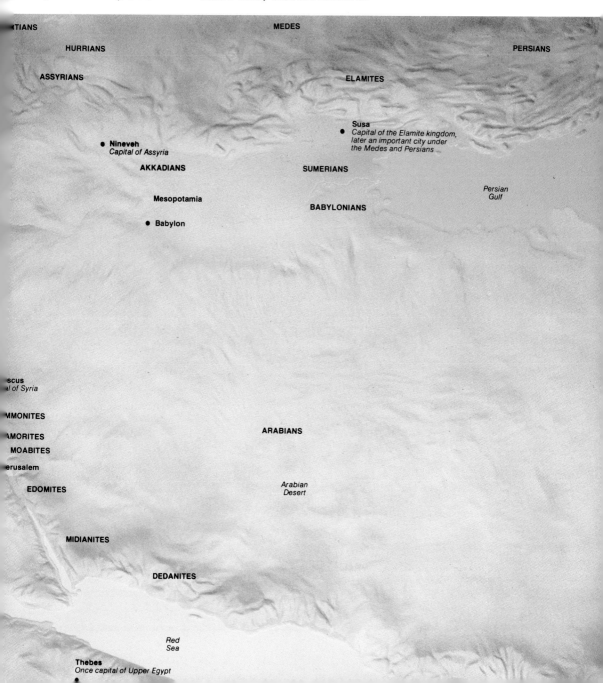

TIANS

HURRIANS

ASSYRIANS

MEDES

PERSIANS

ELAMITES

● **Nineveh**
Capital of Assyria

Susa
● *Capital of the Elamite kingdom, later an important city under the Medes and Persians*

AKKADIANS

SUMERIANS

Persian Gulf

Mesopotamia

BABYLONIANS

● **Babylon**

scus
l of Syria

MMONITES

AMORITES

MOABITES

erusalem

EDOMITES

ARABIANS

Arabian Desert

MIDIANITES

DEDANITES

Red Sea

Thebes
Once capital of Upper Egypt
●

The Patriarchs: Abraham to Joseph

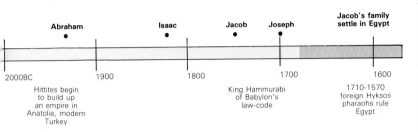

				Jacob's family settle in Egypt
Abraham	Isaac	Jacob	Joseph	
•	•	•	•	
2000BC	1900	1800	1700	1600
Hittites begin to build up an empire in Anatolia, modern Turkey		King Hammurabi of Babylon's law-code		1710-1570 foreign Hyksos pharaohs rule Egypt

Abraham, whom God called to be the ancestor of a great nation, came from the south Mesopotamian city of Ur. Some of his family settled at Harran in the north while he went on to Canaan, in obedience to God's command.

The world of Israel's early ancestors was one of rich and powerful kingdoms in the river valleys of Egypt and Mesopotamia. In the lands between were many walled cities and tiny kingdoms. These strongholds protected the settlers who farmed the country around. But there were also nomadic tribes who moved from place to place in search of good grazing for their flocks and herds. Abraham and his family were just one group among many on the move in the area.

This was the pattern in Canaan when Abraham arrived to set up camp at Shechem. The coastal plain and the Jordan Valley, where there was good farm land, were already settled. This looked attractive to Abraham's nephew Lot, who moved down from the hills to camp near Sodom. But life there had its dangers. Lot was only one of many who suffere when rebel kings tried to throv off the control of their distant overlords (Genesis 14).

☐ Abraham

Abraham spent most of his life in Canaan (the land God promised to give to him and his descendants), based near Hebron, apart from a brief visit to Egypt at a time of famine. At long last the prom ised son, Isaac, was born. Bu Abraham never owned the land. When his wife Sarah di he had to buy ground from a Hittite to bury her. **(Map 1)**

☐ Jacob

Abraham's grandson Jacob, having cheated his brother Es out of his inheritance, left on a hurried visit to relations in Paddan-aram, the district around Harran. For twenty years he worked for his wily uncle Laban. Then he took h two wives and their children, his flocks and herds, and returned home. Jacob was still very much afraid of Esau's anger and at Mahanaim he

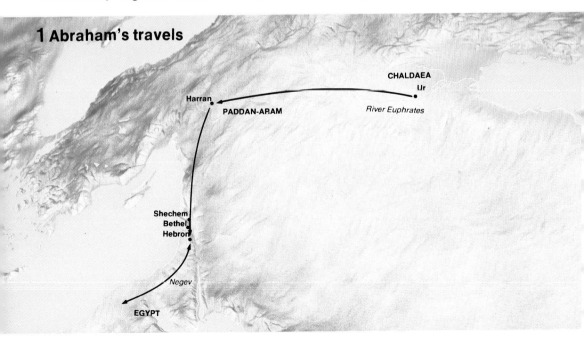

1 Abraham's travels

CHALDAEA
Ur
Harran
PADDAN-ARAM
River Euphrates
Shechem
Bethel
Hebron
Negev
EGYPT

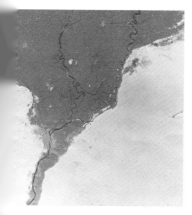

This satellite picture of the Nile Delta, Egypt (photographed on infra-red film) shows as red the crops, trees and plants of the fertile area. Suburban areas, with sparse vegetation, appear as light pink, the desert as light grey, cities dark grey, the waters of the River Nile as blue-black.

prayed desperately for God's help. Reassurance came and the reunion was a friendly one. The rest of Jacob's life was spent in Canaan until in his old age he joined Joseph in Egypt. **(Map 2)**

☐ Joseph

Joseph's position as Jacob's favourite son, and his boasting, earned his brothers' hatred. When the opportunity came, they sold him into slavery. In Egypt Joseph rose to high position. He was imprisoned on a false charge, but eventually became one of the king of Egypt's chief ministers.

Drought and famine often struck Canaan. In Egypt Joseph ensured that grain was stored. His brothers came to buy corn, and the whole family eventually settled in Goshen, in the eastern Nile Delta, near to the court. This is where the Book of Genesis ends. **(Map 3)**

Two pictures of Harran today. Here, over 600 miles/960 km north-west of Ur, Abraham broke his journey and some of the family settled.

2 Jacob's journey, and his return home

GILEAD

Shechem
Penuel
Succoth Mahanaim

Bethel

Ephrath
(Bethlehem)

Hebron
(Kiriath-arba)

Esau comes
from Edom
to meet his
brother

3 Joseph and his family go to Egypt

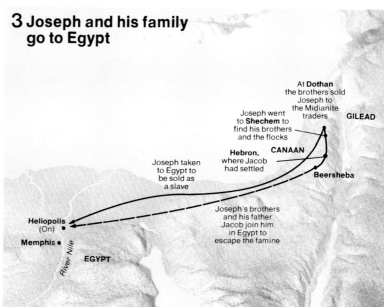

At **Dothan**
the brothers sold
Joseph to
the Midianite
Joseph went traders **GILEAD**
to **Shechem** to
find his brothers
and the flocks

Hebron, **CANAAN**
where Jacob
had settled

Joseph taken
to Egypt to
be sold as
a slave

Beersheba

Heliopolis
(On) •

Joseph's brothers
and his father
Jacob join him
in Egypt to
escape the famine

Memphis •

River Nile

EGYPT

From Egypt to the Promised Land

Pharaoh Ramesses II is generally thought to have been the pharaoh of the exodus.

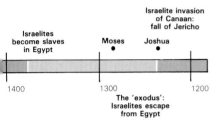

For nearly 400 years Jacob's people remained in Egypt. During that time they had grown into a nation – the nation of Israel. The Egyptians, now ruled by a less friendly dynasty of kings, began to see these people as a threat. They tightened their control, forcing the Israelites to work as slaves in the brickfields. To reduce their growing numbers, new-born Hebrew babies were drowned in the Nile. The people cried out to God – and he sent them a leader: Moses. The date was probably early in the thirteenth century BC, about the time when Ramesses II was king of Egypt.

It took a series of terrible plagues before the king of Egypt would agree to let the Israelites leave his country. Time and again he refused. It was the tenth plague that gained Israel's freedom, and this was something different.

'All through Egypt,' Moses announced, 'on a certain night, the firstborn sons in every household will die.' The firstborn sons of the Hebrews would be safe if the people carefully followed the instruc-tions Moses gave them. They must mark their doorposts with the blood of a lamb killed in sacrifice. They must cook the lamb (again as instructed) and eat it that night, with bitter herbs and bread made without yeast. They must pack their belongings and get dressed, ready for a journey. It all happened as God said.

Every year afterwards the people of Israel kept the anniversary of this event as the Festival of the Passover: for after this (when death 'passed

Out of Egypt into Canaan

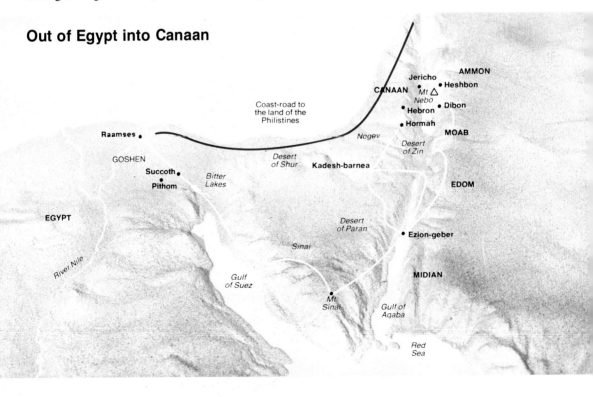

ver' the families of Israel) haraoh let them go.

Even so, at the last minute e changed his mind and sent is army in pursuit – but the raelites escaped across the ea of reeds' to Sinai. The xodus' had begun. The word leans simply a going out or eparture. But this 'going out' f Egypt, *the* exodus, was the ey event in the history of Old estament Israel. All future enerations were to look back o it. Annual religious festivals ommemorated it. Parents were o make sure their children earned what it meant.
xodus 1–15

] The commandments at 1t Sinai

fter travelling for nearly three 1onths the refugees camped efore Mt Sinai, one of the 1ountain peaks in the south of he Sinai peninsula. There, in n awe-inspiring setting, God ompleted what he had begun vhen he rescued the people

The Judean hills seen from the foothills of Moab: the promised and on which Moses gazed from Mount Nebo.

from Egypt. He made his agreement (covenant) with them. He formally declared that the rabble of ex-slaves were his people, the nation of Israel.

For their part they must listen to him and obey his laws, summed up in the Ten Commandments which he gave to Moses on two stone tablets. They set out the basic principles that would govern the people's lives. Their promise to obey was confirmed in a solemn ceremony. Animal sacrifices were offered and the blood was sprinkled on the people and on the altar. So the agreement was sealed.

God then told them how to build a special tent (the tabernacle) that would be the sign of his presence with them all the rest of their journey.

Exodus 16–40

□ Which way?

We cannot be certain of the Israelites' route through the Sinai Desert. Numbers 33 lists many places we cannot now locate. But most probably the people travelled south, close to the coast for some way, then

inland to the region of Mt Sinai.

They moved on to Kadesh and sent spies to explore the land of Canaan. The report came back: the land was rich and fertile, but it was a land of walled cities and giant people.

When they heard this, the Israelites refused point-blank to obey God and go forward. As punishment they spent forty years in the harsh conditions of the desert. Then they took the road on the east side of the Arabah Valley, skirting Edom, to fight their first battles with the Amorites and Moabites. They camped on the plains of Moab across the Jordan from Jericho. Moses died, and Joshua became their new leader.
Numbers; Deuteronomy

Joshua, the Conquest and the Judges

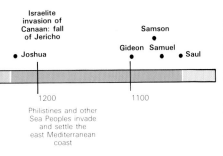

Israelite invasion of Canaan: fall of Jericho

Samson
Gideon Samuel
• Joshua   • Saul

1200   1100

Philistines and other Sea Peoples invade and settle the east Mediterranean coast

Joshua took over leadership of the people when at last (about 1230 BC) they crossed the River Jordan to enter Canaan from the west. In front of them was the walled town of Jericho. The whole land God had promised them was waiting to be possessed.

Canaan at this time was divided into a large number of small independent states, each centred on a fortified town with its own ruler.

☐ The fall of Jericho
Joshua's first aim was to take Jericho, a strategic walled town which was ancient even then, as modern excavations have shown. It fell after a remarkable siege. The Bible describes how each day for six days the whole army marched round the town without a sound except for their tramping feet and the blast of trumpets. On the seventh day they marched round seven times and then gave a tremendous shout. The walls collapsed. The men moved in and completely destroyed the town.

☐ Victory in the south
After an initial setback Joshua took nearby Ai and then marched on to establish himself at Shechem, a key town on the road through the centre of the country. This gave him

a good foothold in Canaan. Enemies remained to the south and north. They were alarmed by his successes and attacked from the south.

The men of Gibeon tricked Joshua into making an alliance with them, so the kings of Jerusalem, Hebron and neighbouring cities made war on them. Joshua came to help his allies and defeated their

The twelve Judges and their victories

4

10
6   7 8

5

AMMONITES

3 11 2
12   9
1   MIDIANITES

MOABITES

PHILISTINES

Barak and Gideon
Judges 4 – 7   • Kedesh
• Hazor

Harosheth-ha-goiim
Mt Carmel △ •   △ Mt Tabor
Hill of Moreh △
Spring of Harod •
Jezreel
Abel-meholah •   • Succoth

Ophrah •

enemies at the battle of Bethhoron. He executed the kings Then one after another he too and destroyed the cities of Makkedah, Libnah, Lachish, Eglon and Debir. When he went back to Gilgal, the south of the country was in his hands.

☐ The northern alliance
News of the Israelite victories travelled fast. In the north, the king of Hazor gathered his allies and they marched out to deal with the invaders. Joshua took them by surprise in their camp by the spring waters of Merom and won another victory. He captured the important city of Hazor and burned it down. (Hazor is another city which has been extensively excavated by archaeologists.)

1. **Othniel** of Judah defeated Cushan-rishathaim
2. **Ehud** of Benjamin killed King Eglon of Moab
3. **Shamgar** defeated the Philistine
4. **Deborah** (from Ephraim) and Barak (from Naphtali) defeated Jabin and Sisera
5. **Gideon** of Manasseh defeated the Midianites and Amalekites
6. **Tola** of Issachar
7. **Jair** of Gilead
8. **Jephthah** of Gilead defeated the Ammonites
9. **Ibzan** of Bethlehem
10. **Elon** of Zebulun.
11. **Abdon** of Ephraim
12. **Samson** of Dan fought the Philistines

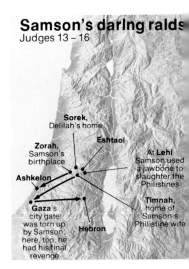

Samson's daring raids
Judges 13 – 16

Sorek,
Delilah's home

Zorah,   Eshtaol
Samson's
birthplace   At Lehi
Samson used
a jawbone to
slaughter the
Ashkelon   Philistines

Timnah,
home of
Samson's
Gaza's   Philistine wife
city gate
was torn up
by Samson; Hebron
here, too, he
had his final
revenge

Joshua attacks Ai

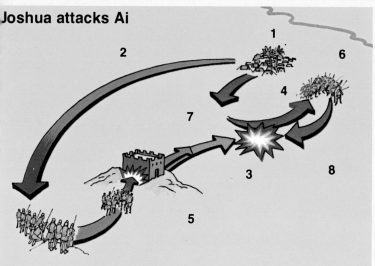

1. Joshua sets up camp

2. Joshua sends his ambush force west of the city

3. Men of Ai advance into the valley towards the Israelites

4. Joshua's main force retreats

5. The ambush force enters and fires the city

6. Joshua sees the fire and signals about turn

7. The ambush force advances

8. Ai troops are caught between the two forces and routed

...le killed the kings who op-osed him but left the other ...ities standing.

Settling the land

...oshua had defeated the kings ...f Canaan, destroyed many ...ey cities – and with them many ...anaanite religious centres. ...he conquest was not com-...lete, but Joshua had done ...nough for the people to begin ...ettling in the land. Different ...arts were allocated to the ...arious tribes, and each tribe ...ad to take possession of its ...wn area.

They never succeeded com-...letely. Enemies remained to ...arass them, and all too often ...he Israelites simply adopted ...he Canaanite way of life and ...orshipped Canaanite gods. ...But there were some outstand-...ng victories (like those won by ...udah: Judges 1) and every-...where the Israelites established ...hemselves in the land. Canaan ...became the land of Israel. Joshua

The Judges

The tribes settled into the areas allotted to them. They were scattered now, and surrounded by hostile neighbours. Joshua was dead. It began to seem impossible to gain full control of the land. Gradually the Israelites lost sight of the fact that God was fighting for them. They began to compromise with the nations around, and with their gods, for the sake of peace. Their enemies took advantage of their evident weakness. The Book of Judges relates the sad story.

The surrounding nations returned to the attack: the king of Mesopotamia from the north: Moabites and Ammonites from across the Jordan; Midianites from the east. The Canaanites at Hazor grew strong enough to make a second attack on the settlers.

And from the coastlands the Philistines pushed the Israelites further and further into the hills.

As at so many times in their history, the Israelites cried to God for help in their need. The 'Judges' won at least a temporary respite. The most famous of these freedom-fighters are Deborah and Barak, Gideon, Jephthah and Samson.

The Israelites conquer and occupy Canaan

Israel's First Kings: Saul, David and Solomon

David's wars
2 Samuel 8; 10; 1 Chronicles 18 –

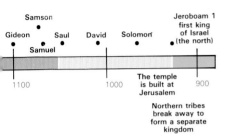

Samson
Jeroboam 1
first king
of Israel
Gideon   Saul   David   Solomon   (the north)
Samuel

1100   1000   900

The temple
is built at
Jerusalem

Northern tribes
break away to
form a separate
kingdom

The last and greatest of the Judges was Samuel – prophet and king-maker. When Samuel grew old, the people asked for a king to rule them, like the other nations. Samuel warned them that a king would mean conscription to the army, forced labour and oppression. But the Israelites insisted. And at last Samuel did as they asked.

☐ Saul

The first king was a tall, handsome Benjaminite called Saul. No sooner had he become king than Saul was faced with a challenge from the Ammonites who moved from the east to besiege Jabesh. He gathered an army and launched a three-pronged attack which drove them off. Following this, and all through his life, there was war with the Philistines. Power soon went to Saul's head and he began to disregard God's clear instructions. Because of Saul's disobedience, his son Jonathan did not inherit the throne. Instead, during Saul's lifetime, God sent Samuel to anoint David as Israel's next king.

☐ David

While still just a shepherd-boy, David killed the Philistine champion, Goliath. His popularity made Saul jealous, and for a number of years David was forced to live as an outlaw, in danger of his life. Then Saul and Jonathan were killed in battle against the Philistines on Mt Gilboa. David was made

PHILISTINES

David defeats
the Philistines
and ends their
control over
the land

Mt Gilboa, where Saul and his son Jonathan died.

Saul's campaigns

- **Aphek** Philistines gather
- **Endor** Saul consults a medium
- **Beth-shan** Saul's body nailed to the city wall, rescued by men from Jabesh
- Battle of Gilboa: Saul and Jonathan killed **Mt Gilboa** Israelite camp
- **Shunem**
- Valley of Jezreel
- Philistines camp at Michmash; raids to Ophrah, Beth-horon, Zeboiim
- **Bezek** Saul sets out from Gibeah, gathers an army at Bezek, and routs the Ammonites
- **Jabesh-gilead**
- **AMMON** King Nahash of Ammon sets out to attack Jabesh
- **Campaign against the Ammonites** 1 Samuel 11
- **Rabbah**

Saul's last campaign 1 Samuel 28; 31

- Jonathan defends the pass at Michmash
- **Michmash**
- **Gilgal** Saul proclaimed king again
- Saul wins further victories against the people of Edom, Ammon, Moab and Amalek

- **Aijalon**
- **Mizpah** Saul proclaimed king
- **Gibeah**
- **Geba** Jonathan kills Philistine commander

- Philistine troops move north to camp near Shunem

War against the Philistines 1 Samuel 13 – 14

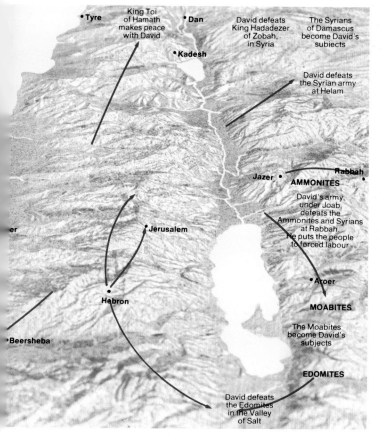

David was made king at Hebron, but for two years he was king only of Judah. At the pool of Gibeon he met the Israelites supporting Saul's family and defeated them. Gradually he won control of the whole country. Then he began to wage war on enemies round about, extending the land in all directions.

...ing at Hebron, but for two ...ears he was king only of ...udah. Gradually he won ...ontrol of the whole country.

David united the kingdom, ...aptured Jerusalem, the Jeb- ...site stronghold, and made it ...is capital. He was a soldier- ...ing. During his lifetime he ex- ...anded the kingdom and drove ...ff old enemies. His legacy to ...is son Solomon was peace and ...ecurity.

Solomon

David wanted to build a temple ...or God in Jerusalem, but he ...ad to be content with getting ...aterials together. It was Sol- ...mon who built the temple, ...nd many other fine buildings.

'Solomon's kingdom in- ...luded all the nations from ...he River Euphrates to Philistia ...nd the Egyptian border. They ...paid him taxes and were sub- ...ject to him all his life.' Peace ...and security freed the king to ...attend to other affairs, among ...them government and admin- ...istration.

A strong, secure kingdom made it possible for Solomon to prosper through trade alliances. His wisdom was legendary. At Solomon's court there was leisure for culture and beauty. His reign was Israel's golden age.

But there was another side to the picture. The introduction of heavy taxes, forced labour and foreign gods sowed the seeds that were to divide the kingdom after his death.
1 Samuel 8 – 1 Kings 11

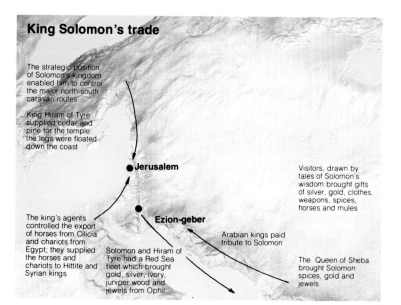

King Solomon's trade

The strategic position of Solomon's kingdom enabled him to control the major north-south caravan routes

King Hiram of Tyre supplied cedar and pine for the temple; the logs were floated down the coast

The king's agents controlled the export of horses from Cilicia and chariots from Egypt; they supplied the horses and chariots to Hittite and Syrian kings

Solomon and Hiram of Tyre had a Red Sea fleet which brought gold, silver, ivory, juniper wood and jewels from Ophir

Jerusalem

Ezion-geber

Arabian kings paid tribute to Solomon

Visitors, drawn by tales of Solomon's wisdom brought gifts of silver, gold, clothes, weapons, spices, horses and mules

The Queen of Sheba brought Solomon spices, gold and jewels

The Two Kingdoms

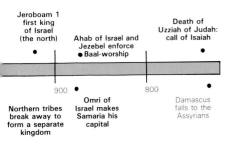

Jeroboam 1
first king
of Israel
(the north)

Ahab of Israel and
Jezebel enforce
● Baal-worship

Death of
Uzziah of Judah:
call of Isaiah

900

800

Northern tribes
break away to
form a separate
kingdom

Omri of
Israel makes
Samaria his
capital

Damascus
falls to the
Assyrians

Under King Solomon Israel became a rich and powerful kingdom, but the people were oppressed and burdened with heavy taxes and forced labour. When Solomon's son Rehoboam came to the throne they appealed to him to lighten their burdens. He refused. The ten northern tribes rebelled. They set up a new kingdom, the kingdom of Israel, with Jeroboam I ruling as king from his capital at Shechem. In the south, Rehoboam ruled the kingdom of Judah (the tribes of Judah and Benjamin) from Jerusalem.

Jeroboam also had to set up a new centre of worship for the northern kingdom, now cut off from Jerusalem. He chose Dan, in the north, and Bethel, an important centre when Samuel was alive. But pagan practices quickly became part of the worship. The historians who wrote Kings and Chronicles classified the kings as 'good' or 'bad' depending on whether they reformed religion or let the pagan practices continue.

Uzziah and Hezekiah were two of the reforming kings of Judah. King Ahab of Israel had one of the worst records. He and his foreign wife Jezebel supported the worship of Baal, opposed the prophet Elijah and persecuted those who worshipped God. The remains of Ahab's 'ivory house' at Samaria can be seen today. Assyrian annals record that he brought 10,000 men and 2,000 chariots to the Battle of Qarqar, where he joined forces with the Egyptians to resist the Assyrian King Shalmaneser (853 BC).

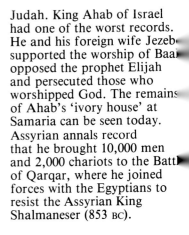

Elisha

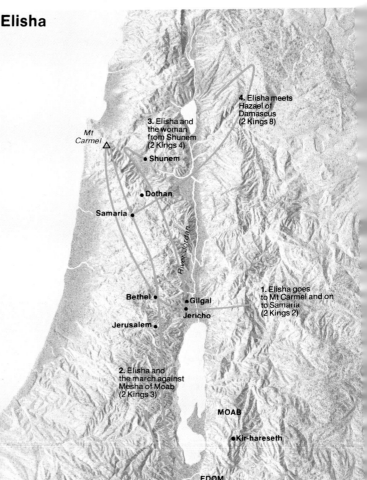

Mt Carmel

4. Elisha meets Hazael of Damascus (2 Kings 8)

3. Elisha and the woman from Shunem (2 Kings 4)

● Shunem

● Dothan

Samaria ●

River Jordan

Bethel ●

● Gilgal

Jericho

1. Elisha goes to Mt Carmel and on to Samaria (2 Kings 2)

Jerusalem ●

2. Elisha and the march against Mesha of Moab (2 Kings 3)

MOAB

● Kir-hareseth

EDOM

Elijah

Zarephath

Mt Carmel

Jezreel ●

Tishbe
Cherith Brook

● Samaria

● Beersheba

To Mt Horeb (Sinai)

The kingdoms of Israel and Judah

SYRIA

Tyre
Queen Jezebel's home

Abel-beth-maacah

Dan
Israel's cult centre in the north

Kedesh

Syrian attack

Hazor

Acco

Chinnereth

Combined armies of Egypt, Israel and Syria march to Qarqar to fight the Assyrians

Intermittent attacks from Syria 900-800 BC (1 Kings 15; 2 Kings 6-7)

Mt Carmel
Scene of Elijah's contest with the prophets of Baal

River Kishon

Shunem
Elisha stayed here

Ramoth-gilead

Dor

Megiddo

Jezreel
Jezebel died here

Mt Gilboa

Taanach

Beth-shan

Ahab (Israel) and Jehoshaphat (Judah) set out to re-capture Ramoth-gilead from the Syrians but are defeated (1 Kings 22)

Ibleam

ISRAEL

Dothan

Samaria
Capital of Israel

Tirzah

Jabesh-gilead

Penuel

Succoth

Mahanaim

Shechem
Israel's first capital

River Jordan

Joppa

Aphek

Shiloh

Bethel
Israel's southern cult centre

AMMON

Mizpah

Ramah

Gibeon

Geba

Gilgal

Gezer

Jericho

Ekron

Aijalon

Gibeah

Jerusalem
Capital of Judah

Ashdod

Bethlehem

Beth-shemesh
Here Jehoash of Israel defeated Amaziah of Judah

Tekoa

PHILISTIA

kelon

Gath

Lachish

Mareshah

River Arnon

za

Here Amaziah of Judah died

Hebron

Ziph

En-gedi

JUDAH

MOAB

Gerar

Zerah the thiopian attacks Judah; King Asa defeats him at Mareshah (2 Chronicles 14)

Beersheba

Joram (Israel) and Jehoshaphat (Judah) march against Mesha of Moab (2 Kings 3)

Shishak of Egypt attacks Jerusalem (1 Kings 14.25)

Kir-hareseth

EDOM

The Rise of Assyria

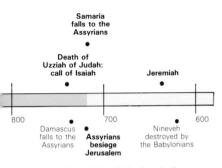

Samaria falls to the Assyrians

Death of Uzziah of Judah: call of Isaiah

Jeremiah

800   700   600

Damascus falls to the Assyrians

Assyrians besiege Jerusalem

Nineveh destroyed by the Babylonians

Israel and Judah, in their strategic position between Egypt and the Mesopotamian powers, were very vulnerable to aggression. David and Solomon were successful partly because none of the larger nations were powerful enough to attack during their reigns. But after the division of the kingdom the nations immediately around – Syria, Ammon, Moab – gave the subsequent kings of Israel and Judah increasing trouble. However, it was the growth of the major powers farther north-east that proved decisive.

The Assyrian Empire had an earlier period of power under Tiglath-pileser I about 1100 BC. But the ruthless aggression for which Assyria was so much feared reached its peak in the period between 880 BC and 612 BC. The empire was based on three great cities: Asshur, Calah and Nineveh.

From the mid-ninth century BC, the time of Ahab in Israel, the kings of Assyria repeatedly attacked Israel. Soon King Jehu of Israel was paying tribute to Shalmaneser III of Assyria. A hundred years later Ahaz of Judah asked Tiglath-pileser III of Assyria to help him fight Syria and Israel (Isaiah 7; 2 Kings 16). He did so and defeated them both, but Judah had to become a subject kingdom of the Assyrians in return for their help.

When Israel refused to pay their yearly tribute, the next king of Assyria took Samaria, exiled the people and destroyed the northern kingdom (722/1 BC; 2 Kings 17). Soon after this, Egypt was defeated by the Assyrians. In 701 BC the powerful King Sennacherib besieged Jerusalem, because King Hezekiah had stopped paying tribute and joined a rebellion, but Hezekiah trusted in God and the city was saved (2 Kings 19).

The Assyrians had to fight many battles to defend their empire. In the next century several provinces regained their freedom. The empire lasted until Asshur fell to the Medes in 614 and Nineveh was destroyed by the Medes and Babylonians in 612.

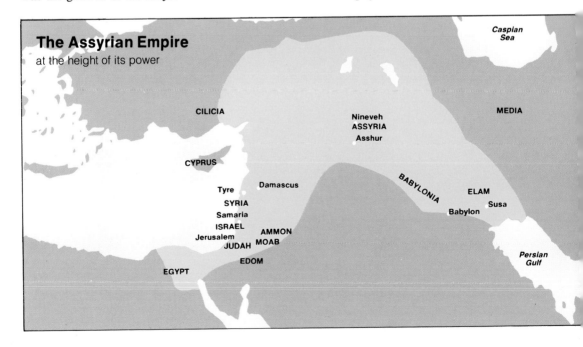

The Assyrian Empire
at the height of its power

Caspian Sea

CILICIA

MEDIA

Nineveh
ASSYRIA
Asshur

CYPRUS

Tyre   Damascus

SYRIA

Samaria

ISRAEL

Jerusalem

JUDAH   MOAB

AMMON

EDOM

EGYPT

BABYLONIA

ELAM

Susa

Babylon

Persian Gulf

Nineveh   **ASSYRIA**

Carchemish

The Assyrian invasions

Phase 1

Qarqar

Phase 2   Damascus

Megiddo   **ISRAEL**

Samaria

Jerusalem

JUDAH

Brook of Egypt

EGYPT

Phase 1
● In 853 BC Shalmaneser's army was confronted at Qarqar by twelve kings who had come together to oppose him: one was Ahab of Israel.
● In 841 BC Shalmaneser again marched on the area, laying siege to Damascus. Jehu of Israel paid him tribute. Shalmaneser then had to secure his northern borders against attack, and Damascus seized the opportunity of attacking Israel and Judah.

Phase 2
● A century later Assyria regained power. King Tiglath-pileser III invaded the area in 743 BC and frequently after that. King Azariah of Judah paid him tribute. The Assyrians increasingly adopted the policy of taking subject people into exile.
● Tiglath-pileser campaigned as far as 'the brook of Egypt' in 734 BC. Then in 733 BC he attacked Israel, destroying Megiddo and Hazor and turning the coastal plain, Galilee and the area beyond the Jordan into Assyrian provinces.
● In 732 BC Samaria was spared only because their rebellious King Pekah was assassinated (2 Kings 15:27–31).
● Shalmaneser V captured Hoshea, king of Israel in 724 BC, and laid siege to Samaria (2 Kings 17:4). He took it in 722 BC.
● In 722/1 BC Sargon II despoiled the city of Samaria, carried off the cream of the population into exile, and so destroyed the northern kingdom of Israel (2 Kings 17:5).

PROPHETS OF THE ASSYRIAN PERIOD

Jonah
Sent to warn the inhabitants of Nineveh (capital of Assyria) of God's judgement. As a result, the people changed their ways and God spared the city.

Amos
Born in Judah but prophesied in Israel during reign of Jeroboam II. Condemned Israel's neighbouring countries for their cruelty, but mostly Israel for breaking God's laws. Warned that the Israelites would be taken captive by the Assyrians.

Hosea
In the years leading up to the fall of Samaria, Hosea warned that the people would become slaves in Assyria because they had forgotten God. They had even turned to Assyria and Egypt for help.

Isaiah
Lived in Jerusalem at the time when Judah was threatened by the Assyrians. Looked ahead not only to the deliverance of Jerusalem from the Assyrians but also to its conquest by the Babylonians and to a future age of peace.

Micah
Warned of the Assyrian and Babylonian invasions; predicted the fall of both Samaria and Jerusalem.

Zephaniah
Lived during Josiah's reign. Condemned the worship of Canaanite and Assyrian gods. Predicted disaster for the pagan nations around. Foretold the destruction and restoration of Jerusalem.

Nahum
Predicted the destruction of Nineveh as a judgement on the Assyrians for their cruel treatment of other nations.

The Babylonian Invasion

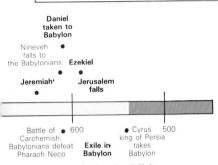

Daniel
taken to
Babylon

Nineveh •
falls to
the Babylonians Ezekiel
• •
Jeremiah' Jerusalem
• falls

Battle of • 600 • Cyrus 500
Carchemish: king of Persia
Babylonians defeat Exile in takes
Pharaoh Neco **Babylon** Babylon

If Assyria in the Bible meant
oppression, Babylon meant
power. Nabopolassar, governor
of the area around the Persian
Gulf, freed Babylon from the
Assyrians and in 626 BC was
made king. He continued to
gain victories over the
Assyrians and in 612 BC the
Babylonians and Medes captured the Assyrian capital
of Nineveh. They were not
content with taking over
Assyria itself but set out to
conquer the whole Assyrian
Empire.

The Assyrians retreated to
Harran but were soon driven
out. The Egyptians, realizing
that their own country might

be in danger, marched north to
support them. King Josiah of
Judah intercepted the Egyptian
army at Megiddo. In the result-
ing battle he was killed and
Judah became subject to Egypt
(2 Kings 23:29). Four years
later, in 605 BC, the Babylonian
army led by the new king of
Babylon, Nebuchadnezzar,
defeated the Egyptians at
Carchemish (Jeremiah 46:1–2).
The Babylonian Empire was
spreading. Jehoiakim of Judah
was one of the many kings who
now had to pay tribute to
Nebuchadnezzar.

After a fierce battle with
the Babylonians in 601 BC the
Egyptians encouraged Judah
to rebel. Nebuchadnezzar sent
troops to crush the rebellion

and in 597 BC, shortly after
Jehoiachin had become king,
Judah submitted. The king an
many of the country's leaders
were taken into exile in Babylon. The policy of the
invaders was not just to
plunder and destroy, but also
to weaken the subject nations
and prevent further rebellions
by deporting their leading
citizens (2 Kings 24:10–17).

Despite this, ten years later
Zedekiah, a puppet king place
on the throne of Judah by
Nebuchadnezzar, appealed to
the Egyptians for help. The
Babylonians invaded Judah
and laid siege to Jerusalem.
The siege lasted eighteen
months. Finally, a breach was
made in the walls. In 586 BC
the city was taken. King
Zedekiah was captured and
blinded. Valuable objects
including the temple treasure
were taken to Babylon. Jerusalem and its temple was
destroyed and the citizens
deported. Only the very poor
were left to cultivate the land
(2 Kings 25:1–21).

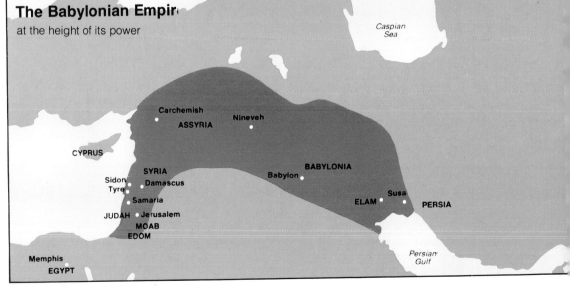

The Babylonian Empir

at the height of its power

Caspian
Sea

Carchemish
ASSYRIA Nineveh

CYPRUS

SYRIA **BABYLONIA**
Sidon Babylon
Tyre **Damascus**
Samaria Susa
JUDAH Jerusalem **ELAM** **PERSIA**
MOAB
EDOM

Persian
Gulf

Memphis
EGYPT

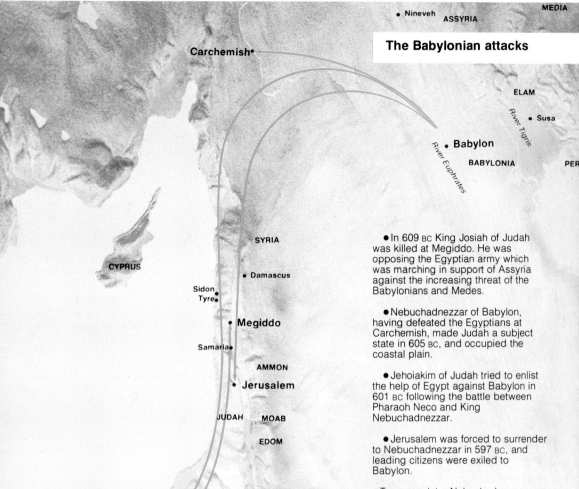

The Babylonian attacks

- In 609 BC King Josiah of Judah was killed at Megiddo. He was opposing the Egyptian army which was marching in support of Assyria against the increasing threat of the Babylonians and Medes.

- Nebuchadnezzar of Babylon, having defeated the Egyptians at Carchemish, made Judah a subject state in 605 BC, and occupied the coastal plain.

- Jehoiakim of Judah tried to enlist the help of Egypt against Babylon in 601 BC following the battle between Pharaoh Neco and King Nebuchadnezzar.

- Jerusalem was forced to surrender to Nebuchadnezzar in 597 BC, and leading citizens were exiled to Babylon.

- Ten years later Nebuchadnezzar again marched on Jerusalem following a rebellion. In 586 BC the city was taken and destroyed, and the citizens were taken into exile.

PROPHETS OF THE BABYLONIAN PERIOD

Jeremiah
Continually warned that Jerusalem would be captured and the inhabitants exiled to Babylon. Prophesied against the pagan nations around. Promised that after seventy years the Jews would return. After the destruction of Jerusalem in 586 BC Jeremiah was forced to live in Egypt.

Habakkuk
Habakkuk questioned how God could allow the cruel Babylonians to defeat his own people.

Ezekiel
One of the Jews taken captive to Babylon. He predicted the downfall of nations hostile to Judah and encouraged the exiles with the hope of returning to their own land.

Obadiah
Prophesied against Edom for attacking Judah at the time of the Babylonian invasion.

Daniel
Taken captive during Nebuchadnezzar's attack on Jerusalem in 605 BC, Daniel became a chief minister at the royal court in Babylon. He prophesied the downfall of the Babylonian and succeeding empires.

The Exile

For 200 years the prophets had been warning that judgement would fall on the people if they refused to listen to God and to keep his laws. In the eighth century BC Amos and Hosea told the northern kingdom of Israel how they would suffer if they did not keep their promise to obey God. They ignored the warning and in 721 BC the Assyrians captured Samaria, their capital city. The people were deported and scattered in other provinces of the empire. Foreigners were settled in the land and it became the Assyrian province of Samaria. The ten tribes of Israel were never heard of again.

In the south, Judah too was threatened, but King Hezekiah trusted God and listened to his prophet Isaiah, and Jerusalem was spared. But the people of Judah only half learned the lesson. The idea grew that Jerusalem, the city of God, was unconquerable. They were safe. It did not matter what they did.

When a new danger loomed – from Babylon – no one listened to Jeremiah's warnings. In 605 BC, when the Babylonians took control of Syria, King Jehoiakim of Judah had to pay tribute. And the Babylonian King Nebuchadnezzar took hostages back to Babylon.

Rebellion resulted in the siege and capture of Jerusalem in 597 BC. The king and many leading citizens were taken to Babylon. The exile had begun.

King Zedekiah's rebellion ten years later resulted in the destruction of Jerusalem and the temple. Those who were not killed were deported to Babylon, leaving only a handful of people. Very little remained of the kingdom of Judah. Settlers from Edom were already taking over the land south of Hebron and Beth-zur. Nebuchadnezzar appointed a governor, Gedaliah, to rule the rest of the country in the name of Babylon. The Book of Lamentations describes the horror of it all. The cities were in ruins. Apart from the thousands exiled to Babylon many people had died in the fighting. Many more died of starvation and disease in the siege. Now few remained to farm the land the invaders had ruined.

Gedaliah made his headquarters at Mizpah and tried to rule well. But some still refused to accept the Babylonian rulers. They plotted against Gedaliah and murdered him. His supporters were afraid and fled to Egypt, taking the prophet Jeremiah with them. The Babylonians carried off still more of the people in 582 BC, and joined the land to the province of Samaria.
Jeremiah 27 – 28; Lamentations; 2 Kings 25:22–26; Jeremiah 40 – 43

Great Babylon with its temples and grand processional way, approached through the Ishtar Gate.

Because of their disobedience to God the whole nation suffered transportation and exile.

☐ The exiles

In Babylon the Jews lived in their own settlements in the capital and other towns. They were free to build houses, earn a living and keep their own customs and religion. They could not go back home but they were not ill-treated. King Jehoiachin and his family were hostages in the king's house-hold. Some Jews, like Daniel, rose to high positions in government service. Skilled Jewish craftsmen were among the workmen Nebuchadnezzar employed. Many became so much at home in Babylon that when the opportunity came to rebuild Jerusalem they did not want to go. But some Jews longed to return to Judah and in exile they clung to their religion and their way of life.

Ever since Solomon had built the temple it had been the centre of Jewish faith and worship. Now it was gone. There was nowhere to offer the temple sacrifices. So the people began to lay new stress on those parts of their religion that they could observe. Keeping the day of rest, the sabbath, became very important. So also did circumcision, the sign of God's covenant with them, and the laws about what was clean and unclean. And they began to value the written records of God's message as never before. Some of the priests, such as Ezra, began to study the law of God in every detail (they were called 'scribes'). Many of the books that make up our Old Testament were given their present form during the time of the exile.

☐ The prophets

Their defeat and the fall of Jerusalem was a shattering blow to the Jews. A heathen king had beaten them. They had lost the land God gave them. Their king, the true descendant of David, was exiled. The temple of God lay in ruins. They faced bitter questions. Could God not save them? Had he broken his promise? Had he given them up? They were forced to look again at all their ideas about God and about themselves, his people. It led to a new understanding.

The answer was there in the words of the prophets. Ezekiel was with the exiles in Babylon telling the people, even before Jerusalem fell, what God was doing. Jeremiah had said the same back in Jerusalem. The disaster was God's judgement on his people for their dis-obedience. They had not kept their part of the agreement made at Mt Sinai. But this calamity was not the end. God had not deserted them. He would rescue them from exile and restore them to their land. Their suffering was helping to prepare them for the new things God was going to do.

See further *The Return to Jerusalem*.
Isaiah 40; Jeremiah 30; Ezekiel 11:14–21 and so on.

The Return to Jerusalem

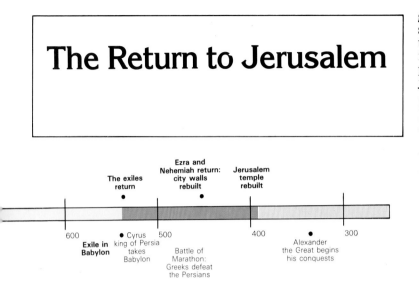

The exiles return •

Ezra and Nehemiah return: city walls rebuilt •

Jerusalem temple rebuilt

600   • Cyrus   500   400   300
Exile in   king of Persia
Babylon   takes
           Babylon

Battle of
Marathon:
Greeks defeat
the Persians

• Alexander
the Great begins
his conquests

In the first half of the sixth century BC Babylon appeared all-powerful. But the prophets spoke of a God to whom kings were as puppets, and who could use even pagan powers to fulfil his purposes.

Cyrus the Persian united the two kingdoms of Media and Persia to the east of Babylon. He conquered lands as far east as India. Then he attacked Babylon. In 539 BC, nearly fifty years after King Nebuchad-nezzar had captured Jerusalem, Cyrus conquered Babylon and took over the whole empire.

The Persian kings extended their borders even further than the earlier empires. They took

Egypt and all of what is now Turkey. When Babylon fell, Cyrus began to reorganize the empire. He divided it into provinces, each with its own ruler, called a 'satrap'. These were mainly Persians, but under them were local rulers who retained some power. The different peoples were encouraged to keep their own customs and religions.

As part of this policy, in 538 BC Cyrus issued a decree saying that the Jews could 'go to Jerusalem and rebuild the Temple of the Lord, the God of Israel'. They were to be given money and all the supplies they needed. Cyrus

gave them back the gold and silver bowls and other things that Nebuchadnezzar had taken from the temple. The first party of exiles made the long journey back home.

□ **Rebuilding the temple**
In Jerusalem Zerubbabel (a descendant of the last king of Judah) and the priest, Jeshua, took charge. Work began on rebuilding the temple. But conditions were difficult. The people had first to build homes and make a living for themselves. Their enemies harassed them. Soon they grew discouraged and work on the temple came to a standstill — for fifteen years.

Then the prophets Haggai and Zechariah spoke out, stirring the people to action. Word came from the new Persian king, Darius, confirming Cyrus's decree and ordering the governor of the province to give the Jews whatever help they needed. Four years later the temple was finished and dedicated with a joyful festival

The returned exiles were still only a small and struggling community, and their city had no walls to protect it. In the reign of King Artaxerxes (464–423 BC) two new leaders came to Jerusalem. Ezra was probably the first to arrive. He was a priest and he brought with him another group of return-

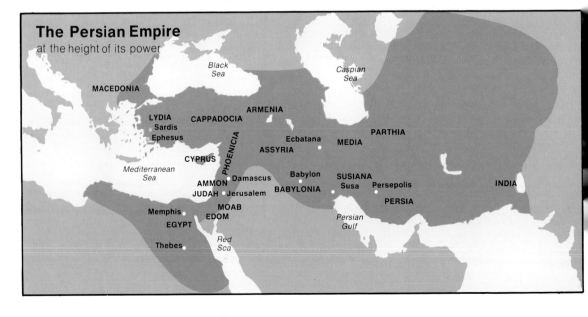

The Persian Empire
at the height of its power

MACEDONIA

Black Sea

Caspian Sea

ARMENIA

LYDIA   CAPPADOCIA
Sardis
Ephesus

PHOENICIA

PARTHIA

Ecbatana   MEDIA
ASSYRIA

CYPRUS

Mediterranean Sea

AMMON   Damascus   Babylon   SUSIANA
JUDAH   Jerusalem   BABYLONIA   Susa   Persepolis   INDIA

PERSIA

Memphis   MOAB
EGYPT   EDOM

Persian Gulf

Thebes   Red Sea

ng exiles. He was naturally interested to see how the law of God was being kept. He found that many, even the leaders, had married wives from the surrounding peoples and were worshipping their gods. Ezra called on them to give up their foreign wives and obey the Lord their God.
Haggai, Zechariah, Ezra

❑ **Nehemiah and the city walls**
Not long after, Nehemiah, another Jew, who was Artaxerxes' wine steward in Susa, heard how things were in Jerusalem and was very concerned. He fasted and prayed, asking God's help. Then he raised the matter with the king, who gave him permission to go to Jerusalem and rebuild the walls.

Nehemiah first surveyed the ruins, and then organized the work of rebuilding the walls. He made certain families responsible for building particular sections.

Enemies from all round Judah did their best to stop the work. They planned an attack on the builders; they plotted to discredit or kill Nehemiah. But the work went on, with some of the men always armed and standing guard. After fifty-two days, 'with God's help', the work on the wall was finished and it was dedicated with thanksgiving.

For twelve years Nehemiah was Governor of Judah, appointed by the Persians. Together he and Ezra guided the community in obedience to God. They made a number of reforms. Nehemiah stopped wealthy Jews charging their poorer neighbours so much for food that they were having to mortgage their land and sell their daughters as slaves. Ezra read the law of God to the people and explained it. They were moved to tears as they realized they had not kept it. In a written document signed in their name by their leaders, the people made a solemn promise that in future they would obey all God's commands and keep his laws.
Nehemiah

❑ **The 'dispersion'**
Many Jews did not return, but remained settled in other parts of the Persian empire. The book of Esther tells how King Xerxes I even made a Jewess his queen.

The 'dispersion', as Jews living in other lands came to be called, was significant later in New Testament times. Because they were away from the temple, these Jews developed the local synagogue as a centre of teaching and worship. And this laid the basis for the later rapid spread of the Christian churches which were formed on this model.
Esther

The Jews who returned to Jerusalem determined to study and keep God's laws.

PROPHETS OF THE PERSIAN PERIOD

Haggai
In 520 BC, eighteen years after the Jews had returned from exile in Babylon, Haggai urged them to forget their own interests and finish rebuilding the temple.

Zechariah
Prophesied to the returned Jewish exiles between 520 and 518 BC; predicted the destruction of nations which had oppressed the Jews; and foresaw a time when people would come from every part of the world to worship in Jerusalem.

Joel
Warned of devastation which would sweep across the land like a plague of locusts, and gave hope of great blessing to follow.

Malachi
A prophet who lived in the fifth century BC. By this time the Jews had become disillusioned and apathetic. Malachi reminded them of God's demands and of the coming Messiah.

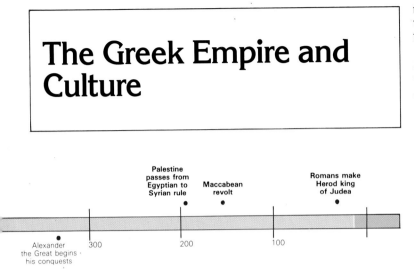

The Greek Empire and Culture

Palestine passes from Egyptian to Syrian rule

Maccabean revolt

Romans make Herod king of Judea

Alexander the Great begins his conquests | 300 | 200 | 100

title 'Alexander the Great' was well earned. He died, when only thirty-three, in 323 BC.

Following his death, the great Greek Empire was divided up among his four generals. The Seleucid rulers, based in Antioch in Syria, controlled Palestine. The Ptolemies, based in Alexandria, ruled Egypt. Culturally, however, the Greek or 'hellenistic' world continued as a unity, with Greek as a common language and with a common pattern of civilization.

King Darius I of Persia (522–486 BC), builder of the great new capital, Persepolis, and conqueror of western India, also pushed the empire westwards. In 513 he took Macedonia in northern Greece and planned to conquer all of Greece.

In 490 the Persians were defeated by the Greeks at Marathon, and the stage was set for some of the greatest stories of Greek classical antiquity.

Xerxes I (486–465) invaded Greece, even occupying Athens, but was defeated in the sea-battle of Salamis. Artaxerxes, Darius II, and the kings that

followed, took up the struggles. The fortunes of Persia and Greece, Media and Egypt ebbed and flowed until finally, in 333 BC, the Greek soldier Alexander of Macedon crossed the Hellespont to begin his meteoric career.

Alexander was only twenty-two when he set out on a campaign which swept across the ancient world. He 'liberated' Egypt from the Persians (founding the port of Alexandria), then marched east, to the heart of the Persian Empire. He pressed on as far as India, conquering all who stood in his way and founding Greek city-states wherever he went. His

☐ The Greek ideal

Alexander's ambition was not simply one of conquest. He believed in Greek ideals and wanted to spread Greek culture and thought. He encouraged army veterans to settle in distant places and build up societies based on the Greek way of life. He was remarkably successful. Greek became the international language. More than 300 years later, when the New Testament came to be written, it was in common language Greek rather than the Aramaic which Jesus spoke.

City-states were built and organized on the Greek pattern, with a strong and lasting impact in Syria and Palestine. Everywhere there was evidence of Greek town-

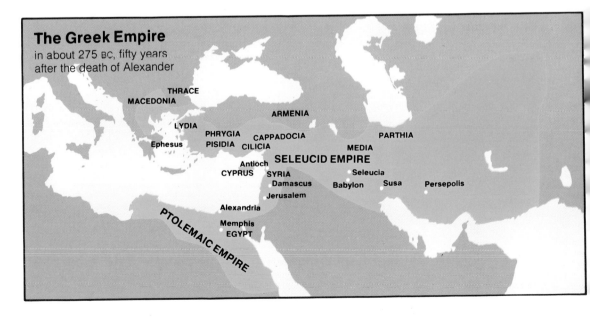

The Greek Empire
in about 275 BC, fifty years after the death of Alexander

THRACE
MACEDONIA
ARMENIA
LYDIA
PHRYGIA   CAPPADOCIA   PARTHIA
Ephesus   PISIDIA CILICIA
                              MEDIA
        Antioch   SELEUCID EMPIRE
CYPRUS   SYRIA   Seleucia
        Damascus   Babylon   Susa   Persepolis
        Jerusalem
    Alexandria
    Memphis
    EGYPT
PTOLEMAIC EMPIRE

planning (still to be seen to-day in many remarkable ruins throughout the Middle East, from Palmyra in the Syrian desert to Ephesus on the west coast of Turkey). Each city had its market-place and public buildings, temple(s) and theatre built in Greek architectural style. The Romans, when they came to power, adopted the Greek patterns which were there already.

Greek thought was as power-ful an influence for change as Greek building. Greek plays performed in the theatres were linked with Greek religious fes-tivals. Paul, a Jew born in Tarsus on the south coast of Turkey in the first century AD, was able to quote the Greek philosophers and poets. Just a few miles from Bethlehem, where Jesus was born, was an area known as the ten towns, the Decapolis: these were Greek city-states.

In the period between the Old and New Testaments Greek culture and thought penetrated deep into Jewish society, even though the Maccabean freedom war won some measure of independence from the Greek kings of Syria who ruled the land. Coins were struck with Hebrew on one side, Greek on the other.

The background of the hel-lenistic world played a vital part in events which were to follow: the events of the New Testament.

Palmyra, a Greek city out in the Syrian Desert.

Rome — and the World of the New Testament

straight roads, aqueducts, plumbing and central heating, and the baths. To the Greek Games were added Roman spectator sports and contests.

The Romans brought law, order and stability to the countries they ruled. The peace was forcibly maintained by garrisons of soldiers whose presence was not generally

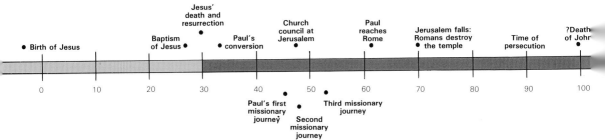

Birth of Jesus • | Baptism of Jesus • | Jesus' death and resurrection • | Paul's • conversion | Church council at Jerusalem • | Paul reaches Rome • | Jerusalem falls: Romans destroy • the temple | Time of persecution | ?Death of John •

0 — 10 — 20 — 30 — 40 — 50 — 60 — 70 — 80 — 90 — 100

Paul's first missionary journey • | Second missionary journey • | Third missionary journey •

The spread of Greek culture (hellenism) and the fact that many Jews were dispersed in other lands had set the scene for the New Testament. The final key factor was Roman rule, which unified the ancient world politically, just as hellenism unified it culturally.

□ **The Roman Empire**
The Romans gradually took control of the former Greek Empire. Corinth fell in 146 BC; Athens in 86. In the first century BC Julius Caesar conquered Gaul and Pompey brought Syria and Palestine under Roman control. He occupied Jerusalem in 63 BC. The Romans absorbed Greek ideas, language and culture. Their legacy to the world was essentially practical: fine

appreciated. Four legions were stationed in Palestine, and there were heavy taxes to pay. The atmosphere was highly charged and revolt – especially where the Jewish religion was concerned – was a constant danger.

In 27 BC Octavian became in effect the first ruler of the Roman Empire. He adopted the title Augustus, and during

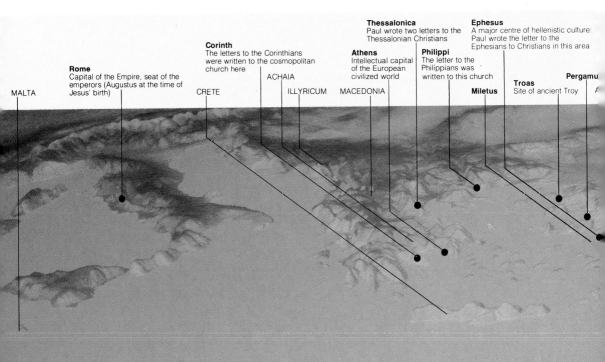

Thessalonica
Paul wrote two letters to the Thessalonian Christians

Ephesus
A major centre of hellenistic culture: Paul wrote the letter to the Ephesians to Christians in this area

Corinth
The letters to the Corinthians were written to the cosmopolitan church here

Athens
Intellectual capital of the European civilized world

Philippi
The letter to the Philippians was written to this church

Rome
Capital of the Empire, seat of the emperors (Augustus at the time of Jesus' birth)

Troas
Site of ancient Troy

Pergamu

MALTA

CRETE

ACHAIA

ILLYRICUM

MACEDONIA

Miletus

...is reign Jesus Christ was ...orn.

When the time was ripe
The time was ripe for the ...oming of Jesus.

The religions of classical ...ntiquity had become bank-upt. The old gods of Greece ...nd Rome had merged with ...he mystery religions, the ...raditional pagan religions of ...he rural areas (the worship of earth and fertility gods) and a general awareness of a world of spirits. After the philosophy of the Greeks and the material-ism of the Romans, people were searching for more 'spiritual' answers: but all too often they simply lapsed into superstition.

In an age of degenerate religion, many non-Jews were attracted to the Jewish faith and became 'God-fearers'.

Because of Roman roads and the Roman peace, the good news could travel quickly throughout the Roman Empire.

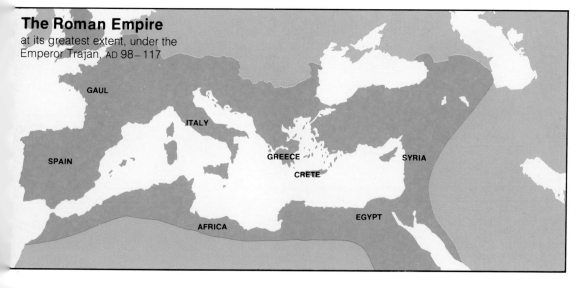

The Roman Empire
at its greatest extent, under the Emperor Trajan, AD 98–117

GAUL

ITALY

SPAIN

GREECE

CRETE

SYRIA

AFRICA

EGYPT

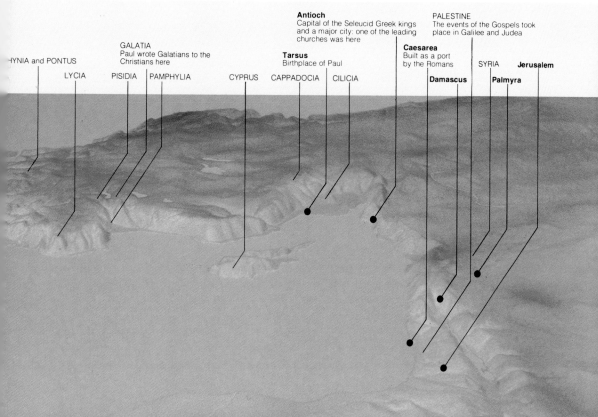

Antioch
Capital of the Seleucid Greek kings and a major city: one of the leading churches was here

PALESTINE
The events of the Gospels took place in Galilee and Judea

Tarsus
Birthplace of Paul

Caesarea
Built as a port by the Romans

GALATIA
Paul wrote Galatians to the Christians here

...HYNIA and PONTUS

LYCIA   PISIDIA   PAMPHYLIA   CYPRUS   CAPPADOCIA   CILICIA   Damascus   SYRIA   Jerusalem   Palmyra

The Jewish Hope

Herod's kingdom

The Jewish people had lived under foreign occupation for some 500 years since returning to their own land. Under Greek rule they had paid tribute to Ptolemy of Egypt and adopted Greek as the language of the empire. In 198 BC the Seleucid Greek ruler of Syria, Antiochus the Great, defeated the Ptolemies and took Palestine. But he in turn was defeated by the Romans at Magnesia in 190 BC.

The Romans taxed the Seleucid Empire harshly, and they in turn took any opportunity to loot cities and temples. Antiochus Epiphanes used the opposition of loyal Jews, the 'Hasidim' or 'pious ones', as an excuse to plunder the Jerusalem temple. Later he built a pagan Greek centre in the heart of the city and in the temple an altar to Zeus on which pigs (forbidden under Jewish food laws) were sacrificed.

This final affront resulted in the Maccabean Revolt. The Jews succeeded in freeing themselves for a time and were able to cleanse and rededicate the temple in 165 BC. The high priest Aristobolus, a later member of the Hasmonean family who had led the revolt, declared himself king in 104 BC. But before long, rivalries among the Jews gave the Romans the chance to intervene. The last high-priest king was executed in 37 BC.

☐ The Herod family
Judea became subject to Rome under the governor of the province of Syria. But the Jews kept the freedom to practise their religion and had their own ruler: from 37 to 4 BC an Idumean Jew named Herod. Despite his ambitious building projects – including a new temple in Jerusalem – the Jews hated Herod the Great, and he is chiefly remembered for his tyranny and cruelty. (Jesus was born while Herod was still king and it was Herod the Great

King Herod's fortress at Herodium.

who ordered the killing of the children in Bethlehem.)

When Herod died, the kingdom was divided among three of his sons. Archelaus inherited Judea and Samaria but was such a repressive ruler that in AD 6 the Romans removed him and appointed a Roman governor or 'procurator' instead. (From AD 26 to 36 this was Pontius Pilate.) Herod Antipas ruled Galilee and Perea. And Philip ruled Iturea, Trachonitis and the land to the north-east.

❑ Religious ferment

The Jews had to accept the authority of Rome and of King Herod's family, but their loyalty was to the priests. The High Priest had great power. There were also a number of religious parties or factions at the time of Christ. Many priests and a large part of the Jewish Council (the Sanhedrin) were Sadducees — very conservative in religious matters and inclined to political compromise to safeguard their high positions. The Pharisees were religious purists, delighting to keep every detail of the law, but tending to a holier-than-thou attitude.

❑ Revolutionaries

While the Pharisees and Sadducees tried to make the best of Roman rule, the Zealots were committed to the overthrow of the foreign forces. They were the freedom fighters, and at least one of the apostles, 'Simon the Patriot', was a former Zealot.

❑ The Messiah

Although some, such as the hated tax collectors, profiteered under the Roman occupation, many were thrown back on their hope of a Messiah, the Deliverer whom the prophets had promised God would send to set them free. They tended to interpret the promise in political terms. But even so, there were many, like Simeon in the temple when Jesus' parents came to present their baby, who were 'waiting for Israel to be saved'.

It was in this time of ferment, unrest and expectation that Jesus was born.

Palestine in New Testament times.

1 Judaea: Roman province
2 Galilee and Perea: kingdom of Herod Antipas
3 Tetrarchy of Philip

In the Steps of Jesus

Jesus was born, Luke's Gospel tells us, at the time when the Roman Emperor Augustus had ordered a census throughout the Empire. It was near the end of the reign of King Herod the Great. Although Mary, his mother, and Joseph came from Nazareth, Jesus was born in Bethlehem, the birthplace of his illustrious ancestor, King David.

The Gospels make it plain that this baby, born into an ordinary family, was the Messiah, or 'Christ' – the one God had long promised would save his people. Many Jews were ready and waiting for him – though he was not to be the kind of king they imagined.

Jesus' infant years were spent in Egypt, out of reach of cruel King Herod. On the king's death the family returned to Nazareth and a quiet life whose annual highlight was the visit to Jerusalem for Passover. When Jesus was twelve Mary and Joseph took him with them for the first time.

☐ A public figure
It was about AD 27, in the fifteenth year of the Emperor Tiberius, that Jesus' public work began. He joined the crowds that flocked to John the Baptist beside the River Jordan and, despite having no sin to confess, was baptized by John, identifying himself with his people.

Forty days of fasting and testing in the desert prepared Jesus for his return to Galilee and the start of a new life as a travelling teacher. Quickly gathering a following of his own, Jesus soon chose twelve to go with him on his travels. From this time until his death (probably about three years later) Jesus was a public figure.

Much of his time was spent in the area around Lake Galilee. But there were frequent visits to Jerusalem, especially for major festivals. Once at least he chose to go through (rather than round) Samaritan country. And he travelled to the far north, to the district of Caesarea Philippi, close under Mt Hermon. The Gospels name many of the places Jesus went to, although it is not possible to work out a precise sequence (see map).

☐ The last week
Probably in the spring of AD 30 Jesus went to Jerusalem for the last time, to celebrate Passover with his twelve friends. He had made a name for himself as a great teacher, one who cared about ordinary people. And he constantly astonished the crowds who followed him with miracles of healing. His twelve friends watched and listened. Three of them saw him transfigured with glory on a mountain in Galilee. They became convinced that Jesus really was God's Messiah.

But there was opposition which grew stronger and stronger. Jesus offended the religious teachers by his plain speaking. They realized that his claims went far beyond those of a great teacher: Jesus was making himself out to be God. Didn't he claim to forgive sins? Hadn't he said that he and God his Father were one?

In Jerusalem that week the opposition came to a head and boiled over. Judas, one of Jesus' twelve friends, arranged to betray him. He was arrested at night and tried by the Jewish Council, with false charges laid by 'witnesses'. First thing in the morning the Roman governor Pontius Pilate was brow-beaten by threat of revolt into ratifying the sentence of death.

On a hill outside the city wall Jesus died as a common criminal on a cross (like the two who died with him).

A hasty burial followed, in order not to break the sabbath laws.

But at daybreak on the Sunday morning, women coming to observe the last rites found the tomb empty, the body gone. And before the day was out many of Jesus' followers had seen him alive.

Here on the east side of Lake Galilee the Gadarene swine rushed into the lake. In the distance is the place where Jesus fed a crowd of more than 5,000 people.

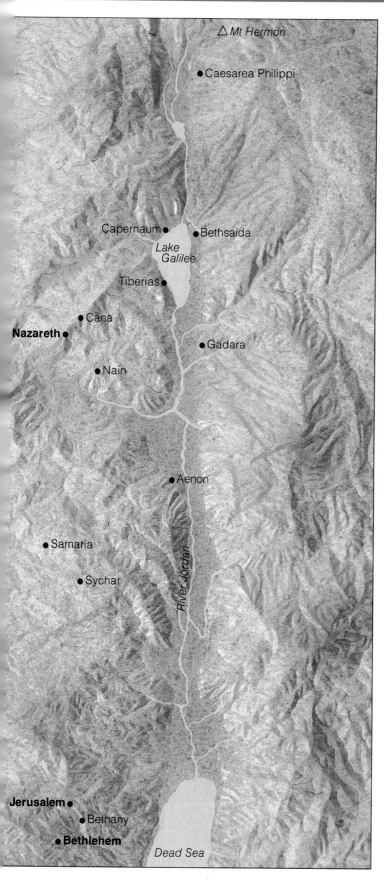

Lake Galilee: four of Jesus' disciples were Galilee fishermen and much of his ministry took place around the lake

Nazareth, Jesus' home town

Pentecost and After: the Spread of the Church

Six weeks after his resurrection, during which time he was seen often by his followers, Jesus returned to God his Father. The disciples were instructed to wait in Jerusalem: they needed the special power of God's Holy Spirit if they were to carry out Jesus' command to make him known. On the Day of Pentecost that power came, transforming the disciples.

The church grew rapidly in Jerusalem under the apostles' leadership. Then the Jews stoned Stephen and persecuted the Christians. Believers scattered all over Judea and Samaria; in towns and village new Christian groups were founded (Acts 8). At this time (about AD 34) two important events occurred. Saul (Paul) the Pharisee, a fierce opponen of the new sect, was converted as he went to arrest believers in Damascus (Acts 9). And in Caesarea Peter preached to a Roman centurion, Cornelius, who was baptized into the

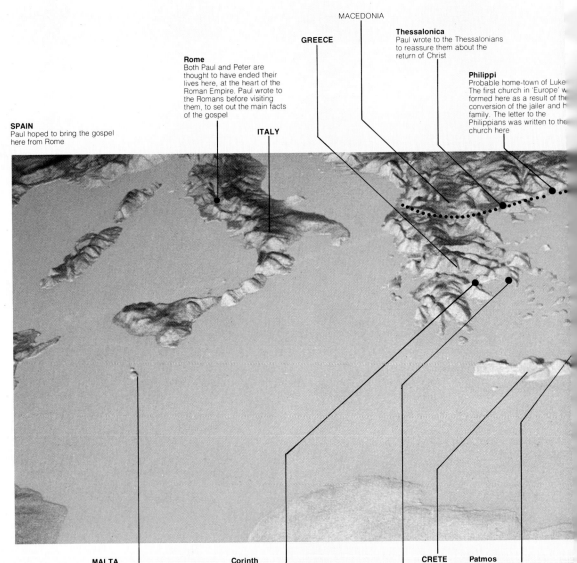

MACEDONIA

GREECE

Thessalonica
Paul wrote to the Thessalonians to reassure them about the return of Christ

Rome
Both Paul and Peter are thought to have ended their lives here, at the heart of the Roman Empire. Paul wrote to the Romans before visiting them, to set out the main facts of the gospel

Philippi
Probable home-town of Luke The first church in 'Europe' w formed here as a result of the conversion of the jailer and h family. The letter to the Philippians was written to the church here

SPAIN
Paul hoped to bring the gospel here from Rome

ITALY

MALTA
Paul was shipwrecked here while being taken to Rome as a prisoner

Corinth
A cosmopolitan port: Paul's letters to the Corinthians show how the church was affected by the current problems of society, such as immorality, idol worship, mystery religions

Athens
The cultural and religious heart of the ancient world and centre for many new cults; here Paul addressed the court convened to settle matters of religion

CRETE

Patmos
While exiled here John wrote the book of Revelation to the Christians on the mainland who were suffering persecution. He included letters to seven churches, listed in the order in which a messenger would visit them

church – the first non-Jewish convert.

In Antioch, the capital of the province of Syria, Christians preached not only to Greek-speaking Jews ('hellenists') but to non-Jews ('Greeks') who had no connection with the Jewish religion. Many became believers; they were nicknamed 'Christians' (Acts 11:19–26). The church in Antioch sent out the first missionaries – Paul and Barnabas. They preached in Cyprus and what is now Turkey (Acts 13 – 14). Non-Jews as well as Jews became Christians. This led to a major problem. Could 'Gentiles' become Christians without first becoming Jews? The conference held at Jerusalem in AD 49 decided that they could (Acts 15). It was a crucial step forward for the church.

Missionary activity increased. On his second journey Paul took the gospel into Europe (Acts 16), about AD 50. His third journey ended in his arrest, but he finally reached Rome in AD 62 and although he was a prisoner, he was able to preach freely (Acts 28).

Many others were preaching the gospel and helping the churches. By AD 64, when the Book of Acts ends, there were churches in all the main centres of the Empire, and from these the gospel was spreading out to surrounding areas.

Colossae
Paul wrote his letter to the Colossians to Christians in this hellenistic city, one of three in the area (Colossae, Laodicea, Hierapolis)

GALATIA
Paul wrote his letter to the Galatians to Christians in this area who were threatened by Jewish legalists

Damascus
Paul was travelling here to suppress the Christians when he was converted by the risen Christ

...as
...e staying here Paul and his ...panions were convinced ...they should cross into ...pe. Troas is the site of ...ent Troy

Pisidian Antioch
Paul visited and re-visited the cities of Pisidia and Galatia, which had been influenced both by hellenistic culture, and the Jewish dispersion: when speaking to God-fearers, he told them about Jesus; with pagans he started from God the Creator

Tarsus
Birthplace of Saul, who became known by his Roman name Paul

Egnatian Way
A main Roman road running from the west coast of Greece to Byzantium

Antioch
A main centre of the church, where followers of Jesus were first called 'Christians'. Paul was sent out from here on his missionary journeys

The gospel was taken east as far as India, according to traditions outside the New Testament

Byzantium

Ephesus
A great hellenistic city and port. ...here was the great temple of ...Diana; the theatre where the crowd cried for Paul's blood; the 'hall of Tyrannus' where Paul taught for two years. The letter to the Ephesians was written to Christians in this district

Alexandria
Later a centre of Greek Christian thought

CYPRUS
Birthplace of Barnabas, so a natural first place for Paul and Barnabas to visit on the first missionary journey

Joppa
Here Peter became convinced that the gospel was for non-Jews as well as Jews

Samaria
The gospel was brought here from Jerusalem to a despised minority

Jerusalem
The church's outreach started when the disciples were given the Holy Spirit on the Day of Pentecost. Jerusalem remained a main centre of the church. The conference to decide how far non-Jews should keep the Jewish Law was held here in about AD 49

Paul's Journeys

Following the remarkable encounter with the risen Jesus on the Damascus road which turned his life around, Paul became the key figure in the spread of Christianity to the west. In the letters to church groups which form a large part of the New Testament Paul refers to his frequent journeys and to the constant dangers he faced. Three of those missionary journeys are fully recorded by his companion, Luke, in the book of Acts – and there was a fourth journey as a prisoner sent for trial in Rome.

☐ Journey 1
The first journey took Paul and Barnabas from their base at Antioch in Syria by ship to Cyprus, and from there to present-day Turkey: Attalia, Perga, Pisidian Antioch, Iconium, Derbe and Lystra. They returned by the same route and took ship to go back to Antioch. John Mark, who had set out with them, returned home from Perga. The date was about AD 45 or 46.

☐ Journey 2
The second journey, a year or two later (AD 48–51), included an 18-month stay at Corinth. This time Paul took Silas with him, after a disagreement with Barnabas about John Mark.

Crossing from Asia Minor to Greece, bringing the gospel to Europe, Paul and his companions landed at Neapolis.

The Egnatian Way, the great east–west Roman highway, brought Paul to Philippi with the good news of Jesus.

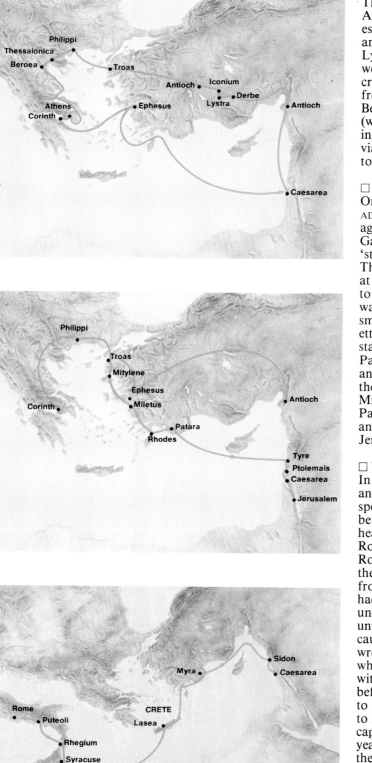

They went overland from Antioch revisiting the churches established on the first journey, and joined by Timothy at Lystra. From this region they went to Troas on the coast and crossed to northern Greece: from Philippi to Thessalonica, Berea, Athens and Corinth (where they stayed), returning by ship from Corinth via Ephesus and Caesarea to Antioch.

□ Journey 3

On the third journey (beginning AD 53) Paul and his companions again went overland through Galatia and Phrygia (Turkey) 'strengthening all the believers'. They stayed for over two years at Ephesus where the response to the good news about Jesus was so great that the silversmiths lost their trade in statuettes of the goddess Diana and started a riot. From Ephesus Paul went to Philippi, Corinth and back, taking ship around the coast from Troas to Assos, Mitylene, Miletus, Rhodes, Patara, then Tyre to Ptolemais and Caesarea en route for Jerusalem.

□ Voyage to Rome

In Jerusalem Paul was arrested and the next two years were spent in prison (AD 58–60) before he finally appealed to be heard by Caesar (his right as a Roman citizen) and set sail for Rome. This fourth voyage, in the autumn, was very different from the rest. Although Paul had Luke with him he was under guard. The ship set out unwisely from Crete, was caught in a fierce gale and wrecked off Malta, where the whole party, having escaped with their lives, over-wintered before completing the journey to Rome. Christians came out to meet Paul as he entered the capital and for the next two years he continued to spread the good news of Christ, though under house-arrest and awaiting trial.

PART TWO

Places of the Bible

Note: This section lists places which played a significant part in the Bible books, with the most important Bible references. The final reference indicates where they can be found – on the Old or New Testament Israel maps in this section, or on the maps in Part One.

Abana Now called Barada, 'cool' One of two rivers which flow through Damascus in Syria. When Elisha's servant told Naaman to bathe in the River Jordan and be healed, the Syrian general despised the muddy Jordan compared with the clear, fast-flowing waters of Abana and Pharpar. 2 Kings 5:12

Abel-beth-maacah A town in the north of Israel, near Lake Huleh, to which Joab pursued Sheba. Captured by Arameans of Damascus and recaptured more than once. 2 Samuel 20; 1 Kings 15:20; 2 Kings 15:29; Map OT/C1

Abel-meholah The place to which the Midianites fled after Gideon's attack. The home-town of Elisha. Judges 7:22; 1 Kings 19:16; Map OT/C4

Abilene The region north-west of Damascus, governed by Lysanias. Luke 3:1

Accad Name of a region and a city in ancient Babylonia, founded by Nimrod. Genesis 10:10

Achaia The Roman province of southern Greece governed from Corinth. Acts 18:12, etc.; Map p. 34

Achor 'Trouble Valley', near Jericho, where Achan was killed because he disobeyed God's command. Joshua 7:24

Adam The place where the River Jordan was blocked, allowing the Israelites to cross into the Promised Land. In 1927 earth tremors caused the high clay banks to collapse at the same spot, and the Jordan was dammed for twenty-one hours. Joshua 3:16; Map OT/C4

Admah One of a group of five cities, of which Sodom and Gomorrah are best-known, now probably under the southern end of the Dead Sea. The kings of these cities formed an alliance and rebelled against four northern kings in Abraham's day. In the battle that followed, Abraham's nephew Lot was taken captive. Genesis 10:19; 14:2

Adramyttium A port near Troy and Troas on the west coast of what is now Turkey. A ship from Adramyttium took Paul and his fellow prisoners on the first stage of their journey to Rome. Acts 27:2

Adullam David, on the run from King Saul and fearing King Achish of Gath, took refuge in a 'cave' (probably a fort) near this town. His family and a group of 400 outlaws joined him in hiding. While he was there, three of David's bravest soldiers risked their lives to bring him water from the well at Bethlehem, which was held by the Philistines. 1 Samuel 22:1; 2 Samuel 23:13

Aenon near Salim The place where John the Baptist baptized his followers. John 3:23; Map NT/C3

Ahava The name of a canal and a region in Babylonia where Ezra assembled the second party of returning Jewish exiles. Here they fasted and prayed for God's protection on their 900 mile/1,448 km journey to Jerusalem. Ezra 8:15, 21, 31

Ai The name means 'the Ruin'. After capturing Jericho, Joshua sent a small force against nearby Ai – and was beaten. The reason was because Achan had defied God's command by taking spoil from Jericho. Achan was punished, and Joshua attacked Ai again. He lured the men of Ai out by pretending to run away, and a hidden ambush force moved in and set fire to the stronghold. Joshua 7 and 8; Map OT/B4

Aijalon An Amorite town belonging by right to the tribe of Dan, but given to the Levites. Much later King Rehoboam fortified the city and kept stores and arms there. Joshua 19:42; 21:24; Judges 1:35; 2 Chronicles 11:10; Map OT/B5

Aijalon A valley through which an important trade-route passed; near to the town of Aijalon. In this valley Joshua fought a great battle against the Amorites, and 'the sun stood still'. Joshua 10; Map OT/B5

Alexandria A great Egyptian seaport on the Nile Delta founded by Alexander the Great. The famous Pharos light-house tower stood at the harbour entrance. Alexandria was the capital of Egypt under the Ptolemies, and remained a great centre of learning and trade.

In Roman times grain-ships loaded up at Alexandria so that the people of Rome could have cheap bread. The city had a 'museum' of arts and sciences and a famous library containing thousands of papyrus scrolls. There was a strong Jewish community, and it was here that the Old Testament was translated into Greek – the Septuagint version. Apollos, who became an important teacher in the early church, came from Alexandria. Acts 6:9; 18:24; 27:6; 28:11

Ammon A state on the east of the Jordan whose capital was Rabbah (modern Amman). See *Rabbah, Ammonites.*

Amphipolis A town on Paul's route through northern Greece on his second missionary journey. Acts 17:1

Anathoth A town 3 miles/4 km north of Jerusalem belonging to the Levites. The birthplace of Jeremiah. Joshua 21:18; Jeremiah 1:1; Map OT/B5

Antioch ('Pisidian') A city in the heart of Asia Minor (present-day Turkey) visited by Paul and Barnabas on their first missionary journey. They preached first in the synagogue, but when non-Jews responded to Paul's message the Jews stirred up trouble and threw Paul and Barnabas out of the city. Two or three years later, Paul visited Antioch again, on his second missionary journey, to encourage the Christians in their new faith. Acts 13:14–52; Map p. 37

Antioch in Syria (modern Antakya, on the Syrian border of Turkey). The most famous of sixteen cities with this name, founded by one of Alexander's generals in honour of his father. Antioch, on the River Orontes, had its own sea-port. Under the Romans it became the capital of the province of Syria and third largest city of the Empire, renowned for its culture. It had a large Jewish community. After the death of Stephen, persecuted Christians fled the 300 miles/483 km from Jerusalem to Antioch.

This was the start of one of the largest and most active of the early Christian churches. Many local people were converted, including a large number of Greeks, and it was here that they were first called 'Christians'.

Barnabas, who had been sent from Jerusalem to find out what was happening, set off to find Paul and ask him to help teach the new converts. They taught together in Antioch for over a year. Some time later the church at Antioch sent Paul and Barnabas out to teach in Cyprus and beyond. Antioch remained Paul's base, and for a long time the church there was second only to Jerusalem. The ancient city was levelled by an earthquake in AD 526. Acts 11:19–26; 13:1; 15:35; Map p. 37

Antipatris A town rebuilt by King Herod and named in honour of his father, Antipater. When Paul's life was threatened he was taken under escort from Jerusalem to Caesarea on the coast. On the way they spent the night at Antipatris. Acts 23:31; Map p. 31

Aphek The Philistines camped at Aphek before the battle in which they captured the Covenant Box (ark) from the Israelites. Eli's sons took the ark to the Israelite camp. Both were killed in the battle, and Eli fell to his death when he heard the news. Much later Aphek became Antipatris. 1 Samuel 4:1; Map OT/B4

Ar Capital of Moab, on the River Arnon. During their time in the desert after leaving Egypt the Israelites were told to leave this city in peace. God had given it to the Moabites, Lot's descendants. Numbers 21:15; Deuteronomy 2:9; Isaiah 15:1; Map OT/C6

rabah The rift valley of
e River Jordan,
retching from Lake
alilee in the north to the
ead Sea in the south and
ontinuing on to the Gulf of
qaba. The 'Sea of
rabah' is the Dead Sea.

rad A Canaanite city in
e Negev captured and
ccupied by the Israelites.
ecent excavations of Tell
rad have revealed an
raelite temple and
ortresses.
oshua 12:14; Map OT/B6

ram A group name for
arious states in southern
yria, especially
amascus. See
ramaeans.

rarat The mountain
ountry where Noah's ark
ame to rest when the
ood waters drained away.
he area, called Urartu in
ssyrian inscriptions, is
rmenia, on the borders of
resent-day Turkey and
ussia. Mount Ararat itself
s an extinct volcano
early 17,000 ft/5,214 m
igh.
Genesis 8:4; Jeremiah
1:27; Map p. 7

Areopagus 'Mars hill',
orth-west of the acropolis
n Athens, from which the
Council of the Areopagus
which originally met there)
ook its name.
Acts 17

Argob Part of the kingdom
of Og in Bashan, east of
he Jordan. It was given to
ne half tribe of Manasseh,
and was a fertile region
with many strong towns.
Deuteronomy 3; 1 Kings 4

Arimathea The home of
Joseph, a secret disciple
of Jesus, in whose new
rock-tomb the body of
Jesus was placed after he
was crucified.
Matthew 27:57; Mark
15:43

Armageddon See
Megiddo.

Arnon A river which flows
into the Dead Sea from the
east (now Wadi Mujib). It
formed the border
between the Amorites and
Moabites. The invading
Hebrews defeated the
Amorites and their land
was settled by the tribe of
Reuben. The River Arnon
remained the southern
border.
Numbers 21:13ff.; Isaiah
16:2

Aroer A town on the north
bank of the River Arnon,
east of Jordan. The
southern limit of the
Amorite kingdom and later
of the tribe of Reuben.
Under Moabite rule from
the time of Jehu to
Jeremiah's day. Also
the name of a town in
the Negev, south of
Beersheba.
Deuteronomy 2:36, etc.;
2 Kings 10:33; Map OT/C6

Ashdod One of five
Philistine strongholds in
Old Testament times.
When the Philistines
captured the Covenant
Box (ark) they took it to the
temple of their god Dagon
at Ashdod. Next morning
they discovered the statue
of Dagon flat on its face;
the following day it was
broken in pieces. Ashdod
fell to King Uzziah of
Judah in Isaiah's time. In
New Testament times the
city (called Azotus) was
restored by King Herod.
1 Samuel 5; 2 Chronicles
26:6; Isaiah 20:1, etc.;
Acts 8:40; Map OT/A5

Ashkelon An ancient city
on the coast of Israel,
between Jaffa and Gaza.
It became one of the main
strongholds of the
Philistines. Samson made
a raid on Ashkelon, killing
thirty men to pay what he
owed in a bet. In the
centuries that followed,
Ashkelon was ruled in turn
by Assyria, Babylonia and
Tyre. Herod the Great,
king at the time Jesus
was born, was born at
Ashkelon.
Judges 1:18; 14:19;
1 Samuel 6:17; Jeremiah
47:5–7, etc.; Map OT/A5

**Ashtaroth/Ashteroth-
karnaim** A city east of the
Jordan, named after the
Canaanite mother-
goddess. It was captured
by Chedorlaomer in
Abraham's time and later
became a capital of King
Og of Bashan. One of the
cities given to the Levites.
Genesis 14:5;
Deuteronomy 1:4;
1 Chronicles 6:71;
Map OT/D2

Asia The western part of
Asia Minor (modern
Turkey) including a
number of important Greek
city-states. Later the
Roman province of Asia,
including the whole west
coast, whose most
important city was
Ephesus. Much of Paul's
missionary work took place
in this region.
Acts 2:9; 19:10; Revelation
1:4, 11; Map p. 35

Assos The sea-port in the
north-west of modern
Turkey from which Paul
sailed on his last journey to
Jerusalem. Acts 20:13

Assyria An important
country in north
Mesopotamia. Assyria was
a great power from the
ninth to the seventh
century BC.

Ataroth A town east of the
Jordan, given to the tribe
of Reuben.
Numbers 32:3, 34; Map
OT/C5

Athens The capital of
modern Greece which first
became important in the
sixth century BC. The city
was at the height of its
greatness in the fifth
century BC when its most
famous public buildings,
including the Parthenon,
were built. Athens was
then a model democracy
and centre of the arts,
attracting playwrights,
historians, philosophers
and scientists from all over
Greece. In 86 BC the city
was besieged and stripped
by the Romans.

Although it lost its power
and wealth as a centre of
trade Athens still had a
great name for learning
about AD 50 when Paul
arrived on his second
missionary journey,
preaching about Jesus
and the resurrection. The
Athenians loved a
discussion and called
him to speak before their
council. Paul used their
altar, dedicated 'To an
Unknown God', as his
starting-point. He spoke
about the God who made
the world and is near to
each one of us.
Acts 17:15–34; Map p. 34

Attalia Modern Antalya, a
port of Pamphylia on the
south coast of Turkey,
used by Paul on his first
missionary journey.
Acts 14:25; Map p. 36

Azekah The town to which
Joshua pursued the
Amorites; later a fortified
border city of Judah.
Joshua 10:10; Jeremiah
34:7

Babel (predecessor of
ancient Babylon) After the
flood, when people still
spoke one language, they
planned to build a city on
the plain of Shinar (Sumer)
in the land of the two rivers
(Mesopotamia) – and a
tower that would reach to
heaven. God saw their
pride and brought the
work to a standstill by
confusing their language,
so that they could not
understand one another.
Genesis 10:10; 11:1–9

Babylon A city on the
River Euphrates,
50 miles/80 km south of
modern Baghdad. Babylon
was founded by Nimrod
'the mighty hunter'. It later
became the capital of
Babylonia and the
Babylonian Empire. About
1750 BC, Hammurabi, one
of the early kings of
Babylon, wrote down on
stone a great code of laws
which it is interesting to
compare with the later laws
of Moses.

After the defeat of
Assyria in 612 BC Babylon
became capital of a
powerful empire extending
from the Persian Gulf to
the Mediterranean. In 597
and 586 BC King
Nebuchadnezzar of
Babylon conquered
rebellious Jerusalem. On
each occasion, many of
the people of Judah were
taken into exile to Babylon
– among them the
prophets Ezekiel and
Daniel.

The city covered a huge
area on both banks of the
Euphrates. Both inner and
outer city were protected
by double brick walls
11–25 ft/3–7 m thick. Eight
great gates led to the inner
city, and there were fifty
temples. The 'hanging
gardens' of Babylon was
one of the wonders of
the ancient world. These
were terraces on different
levels laid out with palms
and many other trees
and plants, providing
colour and shade in a
flat land.

In 539 BC the Persians,
under Cyrus, took the city.
Herodotus, the Greek
historian, says they
diverted the River
Euphrates and marched
along the dried-up river
bed to enter the city. From
that time on, Babylon
declined. Nothing remains
today but a series of
widely scattered mounds,
for the archaeologists to
work on.
Genesis 10:10; 2 Kings
24:1; 25:7–13; Isaiah
14:1–23; Daniel 1 – 6;
Map p. 7

Bashan A fertile region
east of Lake Galilee,
famous for its cattle, sheep
and strong oak trees. On
their way from Egypt to
Canaan the Israelites
defeated King Og of
Bashan, and his land was
given to the tribe of
Manasseh.
Deuteronomy 3; Psalm
22:12; Isaiah 2:13; Map
OT/C2

Beersheba The
southernmost town to
belong to the Israelites, on

the edge of the Negev Desert, and on the trade route to Egypt. The well (be'er) which gave the town its name was dug by Abraham. Hagar came near to death in the desert of Beersheba. It was from this place that Abraham set out to offer up Isaac. Isaac himself was living here when Jacob left for Harran. Beersheba is also mentioned in connection with Elijah and Amos. The phrase 'from Dan to Beersheba' became a common way to speak of the whole land, from north to south.
Genesis 21:14, 30–32; 26: 23–33; 1 Kings 19:3; Amos 5:5; Map OT/A6

Beroea A city in northern Greece (Macedonia), 50 miles/80 km from Thessalonica. Paul preached here on his second missionary journey. The Beroeans welcomed him because they studied the Scriptures. But Jews from Thessalonica stirred up the mob against him and he had to leave. But Silas and Timothy stayed behind to teach the Beroeans more about the Christian faith.
Acts 17:10–15; 20:4; Map p. 37

Bethany A village about 2 miles/3 km from Jerusalem on the far side of the Mount of Olives, and on the road to Jericho. Mary, Martha and Lazarus lived here, and Jesus stayed with them when he visited Jerusalem. Jesus raised Lazarus from the grave at Bethany. He ascended to heaven from a place nearby.
Matthew 26:6–13; Luke 10:38–42; 24:50; John 11; 12:1–9; Map NT/B5

Bethel A place 12 miles/19 km north of Jerusalem where Jacob dreamed of a staircase from heaven to earth. God promised to protect him, and said he would give the land to Jacob's descendants. Jacob called the place 'Bethel' (house of God). Centuries later, when the Israelites invaded Canaan, they captured Bethel and settled there.
When the kingdoms of Israel and Judah split up, King Jeroboam of Israel set up an altar and golden calf at Bethel, so that people could worship there instead of at Jerusalem. The prophets

condemned this, and when the Israelites were taken into exile Bethel was settled by Assyrians. When the exiles returned, some of them lived in Bethel.
Genesis 28:10–22; Judges 1:22–26; 20:18; 1 Kings 12:26–30; 2 Kings 2; 17:28; Nehemiah 11:31; Map OT/B4

Bethesda/Bethzatha A large pool in Jerusalem. At the time of Jesus it was sheltered by five porches, and it is probably the five-porched pool that has been unearthed by archaeologists in the north-east of the city. The pool was fed by a spring which bubbled up from time to time. Many sick people gathered there, hoping to be healed if they were first into the water after this bubbling. It was here that Jesus healed a man who had been ill for thirty-eight years.
John 5:1–15

Beth-horon (Upper and Lower) These two towns controlled the Valley of Aijalon and the ancient trade-route which passed through it. Many armies took this route in Bible times. Here Joshua pursued the Amorite kings who had attacked the town of Gibeon. Philistines, Egyptians and Syrians also came here.
Joshua 16:3–5; 10:10; 1 Samuel 13:18; Map OT/B4

Bethlehem The city of David, 5 miles/8 km south-west of Jerusalem, in the Judean hills. Rachel, wife of Jacob, was buried nearby. Ruth and Naomi settled here. Bethlehem was David's birth-place, and the place where the prophet Samuel chose him as the future king, to succeed Saul. The prophet Micah foretold the birth of the Messiah at Bethlehem, although it was only a small town.
Centuries later the Roman census brought Mary and Joseph to Bethlehem. Shepherds and wise men came to kneel before their baby, Jesus – born in a stable in the 'city of David'. Not long after, jealous King Herod gave orders to kill all the boys in Bethlehem under two years old.
Genesis 35:19; Ruth; 1 Samuel 16; Micah 5:2; Matthew 2; Luke 2; Map NT/B5

Bethphage A village near

A modern shepherd looks after his sheep on the hills outside Bethlehem, the town where Jesus was born.

Bethany, on or near the Mount of Olives, on the east side of Jerusalem. When Jesus came here on his last journey to Jerusalem, he sent two disciples to a nearby village to fetch the young colt on which he rode in triumph into the city.
Matthew 21:1; Mark 11:1; Luke 19:29; Map NT/B5

Bethsaida A fishing town on the north shore of Lake Galilee, near the River Jordan. The home of Jesus' disciples, Philip, Andrew and Peter. Jesus restored the sight of a blind man at Bethsaida, and warned the people of God's judgement. Although they saw his miracles they would not change their ways.
John 1:44; Mark 8:22; Matthew 11:21; Map NT/C2

Beth-shan A very ancient city in northern Palestine where the Valley of Jezreel slopes down to the west bank of the River Jordan. The Israelites failed to drive the Canaanites out of this district. After Saul and Jonathan were killed by the Philistines on Mt Gilboa, their bodies were fixed on the walls of Beth-shan, but later rescued and buried by men from Jabesh-gilead. In New Testament times Beth-shan was known by the Greek

name Scythopolis, and became one of the cities of the Decapolis, the only one west of the Jordan (see *Decapolis*). The modern town of Beisan stands close to the mound of the old site.
Joshua 17:11, 16; Judges 1:27; 1 Samuel 31:10–13; 2 Samuel 21:12; 1 Kings 4:12; Map OT/C3

Beth-shemesh A town about 12 miles/19 km west of Jerusalem, given to the priests. It was near the borders of the Philistines. When the Covenant Box (ark) was returned by the Philistines, it came to Beth-shemesh. But some of the people here were punished for not treating it with respect. Later Jehoash, king of the northern kingdom of Israel, defeated and captured Amaziah, king of Judah, at Beth-shemesh.
Joshua 21:16; 1 Samuel 6:9–21; 1 Kings 4:9; 2 Kings 14:11–13; Map OT/B5

Beth-zur A city of Judah, 4 miles/6 km north of Hebron. Beth-zur was settled by the family of Caleb. Later it was one of fifteen cities fortified by King Rehoboam. Men from here helped to rebuild Jerusalem under Nehemiah's leadership. The place stood on one of the highest hill-tops in the land, and was the scene of one of the great Jewish victories in the Maccabean revolt (*1 Maccabees* 4:26–35).
Joshua 15:58;

Chronicles 2:45;
Chronicles 11:7;
Nehemiah 3:16; Map
T/B6

Bithynia A Roman
province in the north-west
of Asia Minor (Turkey).
Paul was forbidden 'by the
Holy Spirit' to preach here.
But Bithynia was not
forgotten. Peter sent his
first letter to Christian
believers living in Bithynia,
among other places. We
know that this area soon
became a strong centre of
Christianity, for early in the
second century the Roman
governor Pliny wrote to the
emperor Trajan about the
Christians there.
Acts 16:7; 1 Peter 1:1;
Map p. 35

Bozrah An ancient city
in Edom, south-east of
the Dead Sea, about
80 miles/128 km south of
modern Amman in Jordan.
The prophets foretold that
Bozrah would be utterly
destroyed.
Genesis 36:33;
Chronicles 1:44; Isaiah
34:6; 63:1; Jeremiah
49:13, 22; Amos 1:12;
Map OT/C5

Caesarea A Mediter-
ranean port built by Herod
the Great. He named the
town after the Roman
Emperor Augustus Caesar.
Statues of the Emperor
stood in a huge temple
dedicated to him and to
Rome. Traders on their
way from Tyre to Egypt
passed through Caesarea.
So it was a centre of inland
as well as sea-trade.
Caesarea was the home
town of Philip the
evangelist. It was also the
home of Cornelius, the
Roman centurion who sent
for Peter, asking him to
explain God's message. It
was here that Peter
learned that 'the Good
News of peace through
Jesus Christ' was for non-
Jews as well as Jews.
Paul several times used
the port on his travels. The
Roman governors lived
here, rather than at
Jerusalem, so it was here
that Paul was taken for trial
before Felix after his arrest.
He spent two further years
in prison here. From
Caesarea he sailed for
Rome after his appeal to
Caesar.
Acts 8:40; 21:8; 10; 11;
9:30; 18:22; 23:33 –
26:32; Map NT/A3

Caesarea Philippi A town
at the foot of Mt Hermon
and close to the main
source of the River Jordan.

Herod the Great built a
marble temple here to
Augustus Caesar. And one
of his sons, Philip,
changed the town's name
from Paneas to Caesarea.
It was known as Philip's
Caesarea to distinguish it
from the port.
Jesus had taken his
disciples to this part of the
country when he asked
them, 'Who do you say I
am?' The answer came
from Peter: 'You are the
Messiah, the Son of the
living God.'
Matthew 16:13–16; Map
NT/C1

Calah A very ancient city
of Mesopotamia on the
River Tigris, later a leading
city of the Assyrian
Empire. Excavations at the
site, now Nimrud in Iraq,
have unearthed
inscriptions and ivory-
carvings which throw light
on the times of the kings of
Israel.
Genesis 10:11–12

Cana The village in Galilee
where Jesus turned the
water into wine at a
wedding. During another
visit to Cana, Jesus healed
the son of an official from
Capernaum. Nathanael,
one of Jesus' twelve
disciples, came from
Cana.
John 2:1–12; 4:46–53;
21–2; Map NT/B2

Canaan The land
promised by God to the
Israelites.

Capernaum An important
town on the north-west
shore of Lake Galilee at
the time of Jesus. It was
Jesus' base while he was
teaching in Galilee. Levi
(Matthew) the tax-collector
lived at Capernaum. So
too did a Roman army
officer whose servant

Jesus healed. There may
have been an army post
here. Many of Jesus'
miracles took place at
Capernaum, including the
healing of Peter's mother-
in-law. Jesus also taught in
the local synagogue. But
despite all this, the people
of the town did not believe
God's message, and
Jesus had to warn them
of coming judgement.
Mark 1:21–34; 2:1–17;
Luke 7:1–10; 10:13–16,
etc.; Map NT/C2

Cappadocia A Roman
province in the east of Asia
Minor (Turkey). There were
Jews from Cappadocia
among those who heard
Peter in Jerusalem on the
Day of Pentecost. Later the
Christians in Cappadocia
were among those to
whom Peter sent his first
letter.
Acts 2:9; 1 Peter 1:1; Map
p. 35

Carchemish An important
Hittite city from early times,
on the River Euphrates.
The ruins now lie on the
border between Turkey
and Syria. When the
Egyptian Pharaoh (king)
Neco went to attack
Carchemish, Josiah, the
king of Judah, made a
needless attempt to
oppose him, and was
defeated and killed
in the plain of Megiddo. In
605 BC Neco himself was
defeated at Carchemish
by Nebuchadnezzar, king
of Babylon.
2 Chronicles 35:20; Isaiah
10:9; Jeremiah 46:2; Map
p. 19

Carmel A mountain range
which juts into the

At Cana in Galilee Jesus
went to a wedding – and
turned water into wine.

Mediterranean Sea
close to the modern port of
Haifa. The ancient city of
Megiddo guarded one of
the main passes through
the hills some miles inland.
It was on Mt Carmel
(1,740 ft/535 m at the
highest point) that Elijah,
God's prophet, challenged
the prophets of Baal to
a contest. Elisha, who
followed Elijah as prophet,
also seems to have made
a base there.
1 Kings 18:19–46; 2 Kings
2:25; 4:25; Map OT/B3

Cenchreae The eastern
port of Corinth in southern
Greece, from which Paul
sailed to Ephesus.
Acts 18:8; Romans 16:1

Chaldea South Babylonia;
Abraham's family home.

Chebar A canal running
from the River Euphrates
in Babylonia (S. Iraq). It
was by the Chebar that the
prophet Ezekiel, in exile
with the Jews in Babylonia,
saw some of his great
visions of God.
Ezekiel 1; 3; 10; 43

Cherith A desert stream
east of the Jordan. Here
God provided food and
water for Elijah during
years of drought and
famine, until the stream
itself dried up. We do not
know exactly where the
Cherith was.
1 Kings 17:3–7

Chinnereth The Old
Testament name for Lake
Galilee, from a place on its
western shore. The name
is used in descriptions of
the boundaries of lands
belonging to the tribes of
Israel, and of nearby
kingdoms. See *Galilee*.
Numbers 34:11;
Deuteronomy 3:17; Joshua
11:2, etc.; 1 Kings 15:20

Chorazin A town where

Jesus taught, near Capernaum, on a hill above Lake Galilee. Jesus was deeply troubled that these places which heard his teaching did not show any change of heart and life as a result. The site of Chorazin is now a deserted ruin.
Matthew 11:21; Luke 10:13; Map NT/C2

Cilicia A region in south Asia Minor (modern Turkey) which became a province of the Roman Empire in 103 BC. Tarsus, where Paul was born, was the chief town of Cilicia. Behind it, running north-east, lay the wild Taurus mountains, cut through by an impressive pass known as the Cilician Gates.
Acts 21:39; 22:3; 23:34; Map p. 35

Colossae A city in the Lycus Valley, in the Roman province of Asia (now south-west Turkey). It stood just a few miles from Laodicea, on the main road east from Ephesus. The Christian message probably reached Colossae when Paul was staying at Ephesus, though he himself never went there. Paul wrote a letter (Colossians) to the church there.
Colossians 1:2; Map p. 35

Corinth An old Greek city destroyed by the Romans in 146 BC and rebuilt by them a hundred years later. Corinth stood on the narrow neck of land connecting mainland Greece with the southern peninsula, between the Aegean and Adriatic seas. It was a good position for trade.
The town attracted people of many nationalities. It was dominated by the 'Acro-corinth', the steep rock on which the acropolis and a temple to Aphrodite (goddess of love) was built. Temple prostitutes and a large 'floating' population helped to give Corinth a very bad name for all kinds of immoral behaviour.
Paul stayed in Corinth for eighteen months, on his second missionary journey. During that time he founded a church to which he later wrote at least two letters now in the New Testament (1 and 2 Corinthians).
Acts 18; Map p. 35

Crete A mountainous island in the eastern Mediterranean Sea. The 'Cherethites', who formed part of King David's bodyguard, probably came from Crete. Much earlier, from before 2000 BC until after 1400 BC, the Minoan civilization flourished on the island. It was a home of the Philistines.
In the New Testament, men from Crete were in Jerusalem on the Day of Pentecost. Paul's ship called at the island on its way to Rome. At some stage he had visited Crete and left Titus there to help the newly-formed church.
Genesis 10:14; Deuteronomy 2:23; Jeremiah 47:4; Amos 9:7; Acts 2:11; 28:7–14; Titus 1:5, 12–13; Map p. 35

Cush A land in Africa (Sudan) named after the grandson of Noah. The English versions sometimes translate the name as Ethiopia.
Genesis 10:6–8; Isaiah 11:11; 18:11

Cyprus A large island in the eastern Mediterranean Sea. In the Old Testament 'Elishah' may refer to Cyprus, and 'Kittim' to Cypriots.
In the New Testament Cyprus features as the home of Barnabas. It was the first place Paul and Barnabas visited when they set out to take the good news of Jesus to the non-Jewish world. Here they met the governor, Sergius Paulus, and his magician friend. Barnabas later returned to Cyprus with Mark.
Acts 4:36; 13:4–12; 15:39; 27:4; Map p. 35

Cyrene A Greek city on the north coast of Africa, in modern Libya. A man from Cyrene, Simon, was forced to carry Jesus' cross. Jews from Cyrene were among those present in Jerusalem on the Day of Pentecost. Other Cyrenians became involved in the earliest mission to non-Jews, at Antioch.
Matthew 27:32; Mark 15:21; Acts 2:10; 6:9; 11:20; 13:1; Map p. 34

Dalmatia A Roman province on the east coast of the Adriatic Sea, along the coast of modern Yugoslavia. Paul's second letter to Timothy shows him almost alone at the end of his life. His friends have left him for various reasons. Titus has gone to Dalmatia.
2 Timothy 4:10

Damascus The capital of Syria. Damascus was already well known in Abraham's day, and is often mentioned in the Old Testament. King David captured the city, but it soon regained its independence. Damascus was the home of Naaman, who came to the prophet Elisha for healing. The prophet later went to Damascus to advise on the king's health.
Isaiah predicted the destruction of Damascus. And after a series of attacks the Assyrians captured the city in 732 BC, carried away its treasures and many of its people, and reduced its power. From 64 BC to AD 33 Damascus was a Roman city.
Paul was on his way to Damascus to persecute the Christians when he met with Jesus himself, and the whole direction of his life was changed. He had to escape from the city later, when the Jews persecuted him.
Genesis 14:15; 15:2; 2 Samuel 8:5; 1 Kings 20:34; 2 Kings 5; 8:7–15; Isaiah 17; Acts 9; Map p. 21

Dan The land belonging to the tribe of Dan, and a town (Laish) in the far north of Israel. Dan was the northernmost city of Israel, and the expression 'from Dan to Beersheba' meant 'from one end of the land to the other'. When the kingdom was divided, Jeroboam I tried to keep the loyalty of the northern tribes by giving them two golden calves to worship: one was at Dan.
Joshua 19:40–48; 1 Kings 12:25–30; Map OT/C1

Dead Sea See *Salt Sea* and *Arabah*.

Decapolis (the Ten Towns) An association of ten Greek towns gave this region its name. The Decapolis was an area south of Lake Galilee, mostly east of the River Jordan. Many of the people living there were non-Jews, but they joined the crowds that followed Jesus. Jewish Christians fled to Pella, one of these towns, before the war with the Romans in AD 70.
Matthew 4:25; Mark 5:1–20; 7:31–37; Map NT/C3

Derbe A city in Lycaonia in southern Asia Minor (modern Turkey), where Paul preached on his first and second journeys.
Acts 14:20–21; 16:1; Map p. 37

Dibon A Moabite town east of the Dead Sea and 4 miles/5.5 km north of the River Arnon. The Israelite captured it at the time of their entry into Canaan. It was given to the tribes of Gad and Reuben, but changed hands several times in the course of its history.
Numbers 21:30; 32:34; Isaiah 15:2; Map OT/C6

Dor A Canaanite town. Dor joined the northern alliance of kings who fought against Joshua and lost. The town was given the tribe of Manasseh who failed to drive out its inhabitants.
Joshua 11:1–15; Judges 1:27; 1 Kings 4:11; Map OT/B3

Dothan A town on the route from Beth-shan and Gilead to Egypt. Here Joseph's brothers sold him to the Ishmaelite traders. At Dothan, Elisha was rescued from the surrounding Syrian army.
Genesis 37:17–28; 2 Kings 6; Map OT/B3

Ebal A rocky mountain in Samaria, opposite the wooded height of Mt Gerizim, close to ancient Shechem and modern Nablus. Here Joshua carried out a command given him by Moses before the conquest of the land. He built an altar on Mt Ebal and gave the people a choice – to obey God and enjoy his blessing, or to disobey and be punished. Some of the people stood on Mt Ebal, whose bare, scorched height represented God's curse, and others on Mt Gerizim.
Deuteronomy 11:29; 27; Joshua 8:30, 33; Map OT/B4

Eden The garden God made, in the beginning, as a place for his people to live in. After they had disobeyed him, God sent Adam and Eve out of the Garden of Eden. Two of the rivers in it were the Tigris and the Euphrates.
Genesis 2:8–14

Edom The mountainous land south of the Dead Sea where Esau's descendants settled.

Edrei The site of a battle where the Israelites

...aight Street in ...mascus, the place where ...ul's sight was restored, ...oday lined with small ...ops selling goods of all ...ds. Damascus was an important city and centre of trade in Old as well as New Testament times. The inset picture shows a local weaver at his loom.

destroyed the army of Og, king of Bashan, who fought them before they entered the Promised Land. Edrei is the modern Der'a, on the Syrian frontier with Jordan.
Numbers 21:33; Deuteronomy 1:4; 3:1, 10; Joshua 12:4; 13:12, 31; Map OT/D3

Eglon One of a group of Amorite cities conquered by Joshua in his first vigorous campaign. It was probably Tell el-Hesi near Lachish, in the Shephelah, the low hill-country west of Jerusalem.

Egypt A fertile and powerful land to the south of Israel, prominent throughout the history of the Old Testament, especially at the time of the Exodus.
Genesis 46; Exodus 1–14; Map p. 6

Ekron One of the five main cities of the Philistines. It was given to the tribe of Judah in the early years of conquest. But the Philistines on the coastal plain were too strong for them to keep it. When the Philistines defeated Israel and captured the Covenant Box (ark), plague broke out in each of the Philistine cities to which the ark was taken. When the plague reached Ekron, the Philistines finally decided to send the ark back to the Israelites. Ekron remained a Philistine city. When King Ahaziah turned away from the God of Israel, he sent to consult Baal-zebub, the god of Ekron. 'Beelzebub' was regarded in New Testament times as the prince of evil spirits.
Joshua 15:11, 45–46; Judges 1:18; 1 Samuel 5:10–6:17; 7:14; 17:52; 2 Kings 1:3–6; Amos 1:8, etc.; Map OT/A5

Elah A valley south-west of Jerusalem. The Philistines marched through the Valley of Elah to invade the land of Israel. Here David fought the Philistine champion Goliath.
1 Samuel 17:2

Elam The country east of Babylonia whose capital was Susa.

Elath/Ezion-geber A settlement (later a town) at the head of the Gulf of Aqaba on the Red Sea. The Israelites camped there on their way from Egypt to Canaan. King Solomon based a Red Sea

trading fleet there. King Jehoshaphat later tried to revive this, but his ships were wrecked. The town eventually came under Edomite control.
Numbers 33:35–36; Deuteronomy 2:8; 1 Kings 9:26–27; 22:48; 2 Kings 16:6; Map p. 15

Emmaus A village within 8 miles/13 km of Jerusalem. It was probably modern El-Qubeibeh. On the day of his resurrection Jesus appeared to two of his followers who were on their way to Emmaus.
Luke 24:13; Map NT/B5

Endor A place in northern Israel, near Mt Tabor. King Saul made a secret journey to Endor on the night before his last battle. He wanted to ask the witch (or medium) there to call up the spirit of the dead prophet Samuel, to advise him. Saul and his son Jonathan were killed next day in the disastrous defeat at nearby Mt Gilboa.
1 Samuel 28; Map OT/B3

Engedi A spring to the west of the Dead Sea where David hid out.
Joshua 15:62; 1 Samuel 23:29, etc.; Map OT/B6

En-rogel A well on the south side of Jerusalem, near where the Hinnom Valley joins the Kidron Valley. Adonijah, one of King David's sons, had

himself anointed king here before his father's death. He was trying to prevent the kingdom from going to Solomon.
1 Kings 1:9

Ephesus The most important city in the Roman province of Asia (western Turkey). Ephesus was a bridgehead between East and West. It stood at the end of one of the great caravan trade routes through Asia, at the mouth of the Cayster River. By Paul's day the harbour was beginning to silt up. But the city was magnificent, with streets paved in marble, baths, libraries, a market-place and theatre seating more than 25,000 people. The temple to Diana at Ephesus was one of the seven wonders of the ancient world, four times the size of the Parthenon at Athens.

There had been a settlement at Ephesus since before the twelfth century BC. But by New Testament times the population had grown to something like a third of a million, including a great many Jews.

Ephesus soon became an important centre for the early Christians, too. Paul made a brief visit on his second missionary journey, and his friends

Aquila and Prisca stayed on there. On his third journey he spent over two years at Ephesus, and the Christian message spread widely throughout the province. Sales of silver images of Diana began to fall off. People's incomes were threatened and there was a riot.

Paul wrote his letters to Corinth from Ephesus. And some of his letters from prison (Philippians, etc.) are sometimes thought to have been written from Ephesus. Timothy stayed behind to help the church when Paul left. Paul later wrote a letter to the Christians at Ephesus. One of the letters to the seven churches in Revelation was also addressed to them.

There is a tradition that Ephesus became the home of the apostle John.
Acts 18:19; 19; 20:17; 1 Corinthians 15:32; 16:8–9; Ephesians 1:1; 1 Timothy 1:3; Revelation 2:1–7; Map p. 29

Ephraim The land belonging to the tribe of Ephraim.
Joshua 16:4–10, etc.; Map p. 13

Ephrathah Another name for Bethlehem.

Erech One of the great Sumerian cities, in southern Babylonia, about 40 miles/64 km north-west

of Ur. It is mentioned in Genesis in the list of nations.
Genesis 10:10; Ezra 4:9;

Eshcol A valley near Hebron. The name mean 'a cluster of grapes'. Wh Moses sent spies into the Promised Land they brought back samples o the fruit of the country, including a huge bunch grapes from this valley.
Numbers 13:23–24; 32:9 Deuteronomy 1:24

Eshtaol A place about 10 miles/16km west of Jerusalem, on the border of the land belonging to the tribe of Dan. This was the home district of Samson. Here he grew u and the Spirit of God first moved him to go out against the Philistines in the lowlands to the west. spite of Samson's exploit the Danites never occupied their inheritance
Joshua 15:33; 19:41; Judges 13:24–25; 16:31 18; Map OT/B5

Ethiopia This is Sudan, not modern Ethiopia, and is called Cush in many translations of the Old Testament.

The Roman Arcadian Wa at Ephesus in Turkey leac to the theatre. The inset picture gives a performer' view of the theatre, as he made his entrance into the arena.

uphrates In the Old
estament this great river
often referred to simply
s 'the river'. It is 1,200
iles/1,931km long. It rises
eastern Turkey and
ws south-east to the
ersian Gulf. Its course
rough the Babylonian
ains has moved west,
aving many of the
ncient cities which once
ood on its banks now
–4 miles/5–6km to the
ast. The route to Syria
llowed the Euphrates
orth to Carchemish, then
rned south towards
amascus, Israel and
gypt. The Euphrates is
entioned as one of the
ur rivers of Eden.
enesis 2:14; 15:18, etc.;
evelation 9:14; 16:12;
Map p. 7

zion-geber See *Elath*.

air Havens A small port
n the south coast of
rete. Paul's ship called in
t Fair Havens on the
oyage to Rome. Here
aul conferred with the
enturion Julius and the
wner and captain of the
hip, who wanted to reach
more attractive harbour
n which to spend the
inter. In spite of Paul's
dvice they put out to sea,
nd were caught in the
iolent wind which drove
em to shipwreck on
Malta.
Acts 27:8–12

Gad The land belonging to
he tribe of Gad. Part of
he former Amorite
kingdom, east of the River
Jordan (south Gilead).
Joshua 13:8–13; Map
p. 13

Galatia A Roman province
n central Asia Minor. Its
capital was Ancyra (now
Ankara, the capital of
modern Turkey). Several
cities visited by Paul –
Pisidian Antioch, Iconium,
Lystra and perhaps Derbe
– were in the southern
part of Galatia, and Paul's
etter to the Galatians was
probably addressed to
hem. Galatia was also
one of the areas to which
1 Peter was sent.
Acts 16:6; 18:23;
Galatians 1:1; 1 Peter 1:1;
Map p. 29

Galilee The name of an
area and large lake in
northern Israel. The home
area of Jesus and a
number of his disciples.
When his public work
began, Jesus spent much
of his time here.
Galilee is mentioned
occasionally in the Old

Testament. It was
surrounded on three sides
by other nations and
strongly influenced by
them. Most of Galilee is
hilly, but the land falls
steeply to 682 ft/210 m
below sea level around the
lake.
At the time of Jesus
several major roads of the
Roman Empire crossed
Galilee. Farming, trade
and the lakeside fisheries
were the main industries.
Many of the towns and
villages mentioned in the
Gospels were in Galilee,
including Nazareth (where
Jesus grew up),
Capernaum, Cana and
Bethsaida. The lake, which
is liable to sudden fierce
storms as the wind funnels
through the hills that ring it
round, is also a focal point
in the Gospel stories.
1 Kings 9:11; 2 Kings
15:29; Isaiah 9:1; Luke
4:14; 5:1 and following;
8:22–26; John 21, etc.;
Acts 9:31; Map NT/B3

Gath One of five Philistine
strongholds in Old
Testament times. When the
Philistines captured the
Covenant Box (ark) it was
taken to Gath, but plague
followed. Goliath came
from Gath, the home of
other 'giants', too. Later,
when David was on the
run from King Saul, he
escaped to Gath. Soldiers
from Gath helped him
when his son Absalom led
a rebellion against him.
The city was subject to the
kingdom of Judah for
some time and eventually
fell to the Assyrians in the
eighth century BC. The site
is still not certain.
Joshua 11:22; 1 Samuel 5;
17:4; 21:10 – 22:1; 27;
2 Samuel 15:18; 2 Kings
12:17; 2 Chronicles 11:8;
26:6

Gath-hepher A place in
Galilee on the borders of
the lands belonging to the
tribes of Zebulun and
Naphtali. It was the birthplace of the prophet
Jonah. It lay close to the
later town of Nazareth.
Joshua 19:13; 2 Kings
14:25; Map OT/B2

Gaza One of five Philistine
strongholds in Old
Testament times, on the
coastal plain. Joshua
conquered and then lost
the city. The town features
in the story of Samson. He
was put in prison here,
and finally died when he
brought about the collapse
of a great building. Gaza

suffered with the other
Philistine cities when they
captured the Covenant
Box (ark).
The town was an
important one on the trade
route to Egypt. It was
conquered by King
Hezekiah of Judah, and
later by the Assyrian
armies and the Egyptian
pharaoh.
In the New Testament,
Philip was on the road
from Jerusalem to Gaza
when he met the Ethiopian
official and told him the
Good News about Jesus.
Joshua 10:41; Judges 16;
1 Samuel 6:17; 2 Kings
18:8; Jeremiah 47; Acts
8:26; Map OT/A6

Geba Modern Jeba',
opposite Michmash,
6 miles/10 km north
of Jerusalem. A city
belonging to the tribe of
Benjamin. Saul's army
camped here in front of his
capital at Gibeah when the
Philistines held Michmash.
Later Geba became the
northern limit of the
southern kingdom of
Judah, and was fortified
by King Asa. Like
Michmash, it was on the
route of the Assyrian
approach to Jerusalem,
and was resettled after the
exile.
Joshua 18:24; 21:17;
1 Samuel 13:16; 1 Kings
15:22; 2 Kings 23:8;
1 Chronicles 6:60; Isaiah
10:29; Ezra 2:26;
Nehemiah 7:30; Zechariah
14:10; Map OT/B5

Gebal A very ancient
Phoenician city, often
known by its Greek name
Byblos. It was on the coast
of modern Lebanon, north
of Berytus (Beirut). 'There
is still much land to be
taken,' God told Joshua in
his old age. Gebal was
one of the areas included
on the list. Later, workmen
from Gebal helped to
prepare the timber and
stone for building
Solomon's temple. Ezekiel
prophesied against Tyre
and other Phoenician
towns, including Gebal.
Joshua 13:5; 1 Kings 5:18;
Psalm 83:9; Ezekiel 27:9

Gennesaret A place on
the western shore of Lake
Galilee. The name is also
used of the lake itself. See
also *Galilee, Chinnereth*.
Mark 6:53; Luke 5:1

Gerar A place in the
Negev, between
Beersheba and Gaza,
where both Abraham and
Isaac stayed. For safety,

Abraham said that his wife
Sarah was his sister.
Abimelech, king of Gerar,
wanted to take Sarah as
his wife. But God
prevented this.
Genesis 20:26; Map
OT/A6

Gerizim The mountain of
God's blessing, in
Samaria, opposite Mt Ebal
(see *Ebal*). Gerizim later
became the Samaritans'
sacred mountain, the
place where they built
their temple. It was the
mountain which the
woman of Samaria
mentioned as the place
where her ancestors
worshipped. The site of the
ancient Samaritan temple
has recently been found
on a spur of Mt Gerizim.
Deuteronomy 11:29; 27;
Joshua 8:33; John 4:20;
Map OT/B4

Geshur A region and town
in southern Syria. King
David married the king of
Geshur's daughter. Their
son, Absalom, fled to
Geshur after he had killed
his half-brother Amnon in
revenge for the rape of his
sister Tamar.
Joshua 12:5; 2 Samuel
3:3; 13:38, etc.

Gethsemane ('olive
press'). A garden across
the Kidron Valley from
Jerusalem, close to the
Mount of Olives. Jesus and
his disciples often went
there. So Judas knew
where to take the soldiers
on the night of the arrest.
Matthew 26:36–56; Mark
14:32–51; Luke 22:39;
John 18:1–12

Gezer One of the
Canaanite towns Joshua
campaigned against. It
was in the low hills, on the
road from Joppa (on the
coast) to Jerusalem. Gezer
belonged to Egypt for a
while until one of the
pharaohs gave it to his
daughter, King Solomon's
wife. Solomon fortified the
town, with Hazor and
Megiddo. It is the place
where archaeologists
discovered the 'Gezer
calendar'.
Joshua 10:33, etc.;
1 Kings 9:15–17; Map
OT/B5

Gibeah A hill-top town
3 miles/4 km north of
Jerusalem, which became
famous as the home and
capital city of King Saul.
The place had been
tragically destroyed as a
result of a crime committed
by its people during the
time of the Judges. The

site is at Tell el-Ful, overlooking the suburbs of Jerusalem.
Judges 19:12 – 20:48; 1 Samuel 10:26, etc.; Isaiah 10:29; Map OT/B5

Gibeon A town about 6 miles/10 km north-west of Jerusalem. After the fall of Jericho and Ai the Gibeonites tricked Joshua into a peace treaty. Saul later broke this. David's men fought the supporters of Saul's son Ishbosheth at the pool of Gibeon, to decide which should be king. The tent of worship (tabernacle) was kept at Gibeon, and King Solomon worshipped there. The people of Gibeon helped Nehemiah to rebuild the walls of Jerusalem.

Archaeologists have discovered a huge pit at Gibeon, with a stairway leading down to water. Inside it there were handles of a great many storage jars, each one inscribed with the name 'Gibeon' and the owner's name. The town seems to have been an important centre for wine-making in the seventh century BC.
Joshua 9; 2 Samuel 2:12–29; 20:8; 21; 1 Kings 3:4; 1 Chronicles 21:29; Nehemiah 3:7; Map OT/B5

Gihon The name of one of the four great rivers which flowed out of the Garden of Eden.

Gihon was also the name of a spring at the foot of the hill on which the first city of Jerusalem stood. It was then the main source of water for the city. Solomon was anointed king at this spring by the command of his father David, to forestall the attempt of his rival Adonijah to seize the throne. The Gihon spring water was vitally important to the safety of the city and, later, King Hezekiah cut a tunnel to bring the water right through the hill and inside the walls. This tunnel still exists. The water comes out at the Pool of Siloam (see *Siloam*).
Genesis 2:13; 1 Kings 1; 2 Chronicles 32:30; 33:14

Gilboa A mountain and range in the north of Palestine, overlooking the deep Valley of Jezreel which runs down to the River Jordan. King Saul and his army took their last stand against the Philistines on Mt Gilboa. Saul, Jonathan and his

other two sons were all killed there.
1 Samuel 28:4; 31:1, 8; 2 Samuel 1; 21:12; 1 Chronicles 10:1, 8; Map OT/B3

Gilead A large area east of the River Jordan, extending north from the Dead Sea. The tribes of Reuben, Gad and Manasseh each occupied part of Gilead. The region was good grazing-land, famous for its flocks and herds. It was also famous for a gum or spice known as the 'balm' of Gilead. This was used to heal wounds, and also as a cosmetic. Jair, Jephthah and the prophet Elijah all came from Gilead.
Genesis 37:25; Joshua 17:1; Judges 10:3; 11; 1 Kings 17:1; Song of Solomon 4:1; Map OT/C3

Gilgal A place between Jericho and the River Jordan. The Israelites camped at Gilgal after crossing the river, and set up stones to mark the event. From Gilgal they set out to conquer Canaan. It became the site of an important shrine, and was on Samuel's circuit as a Judge. Gilgal is mentioned in the stories of Elijah and also of Elisha, who dealt with a pot of 'poisoned' stew there. The prophets Hosea and Amos condemned the worship at Gilgal as empty ritual.
Joshua 4:20; Judges 3:19; 1 Samuel 7:16; 10:8, etc.; 2 Samuel 19:15; 2 Kings 2:1; 4:38–41; Hosea 4:15; Amos 4:4; Map OT/C5

Gomorrah One of five cities probably now beneath the southern end of the Dead Sea. Gomorrah was violently destroyed with Sodom for deliberate, persistent and vicious sin. Throughout the Bible, Sodom and Gomorrah are used as examples to warn God's people of his judgement. Jesus says that any town which refuses to hear his messengers is in a worse situation than Sodom and Gomorrah.
Genesis 14; 19; Isaiah 1:9–10; (Ezekiel 16:48–50); Matthew 10:15

Goshen A fertile area of the eastern Nile Delta in Egypt. When Jacob and his family went to join Joseph, they settled in Goshen. It was a good place for their flocks and herds, and it was close to Pharaoh's court. In the

time just before the exodus, the Israelites in Goshen escaped the plagues suffered by the rest of Egypt.
Genesis 45:10; Exodus 8:22, etc.; Map p. 10

Gozan Israelites from Samaria were taken captive to Gozan by the Assyrians. The town is modern Tell Halaf on the River Khabur in north-east Syria.
2 Kings 17:6; 19:12;

Great Sea The Bible often uses this name for the Mediterranean Sea.

Greece The conquests of Alexander the Great brought Israel (and the rest of the eastern Mediterranean lands) under Greek control. The influence of Greek civilization, culture and thought was strong in the last centuries before Christ and in New Testament times.
Daniel 11; John 12:20; Acts 6; 17; 18; Map p. 34

Habor The River Khabur in north-east Syria. A tributary of the River Euphrates. The town of Gozan was on the Habor River.
2 Kings 17:6

Hamath Modern Hama, on the River Orontes in Syria. In Old Testament times Hamath was an important town, capital of a small kingdom, and on a main trade-route from Asia Minor (Turkey) south to Israel and Egypt. Hamath Pass, some distance to the south, was the 'ideal' northern limit of Israel. In the reigns of David and Solomon, Israel had a peace treaty with King Toi of Hamath. The town fell to the Assyrians and many of its people were moved into Israel. First Pharaoh Neco (before the Battle of Carchemish) and then King Nebuchadnezzar of Babylon made it their headquarters for a time.
Joshua 13:5; 2 Samuel 8:9–11; 1 Kings 8:65; 2 Chronicles 8:4; 2 Kings 17:24; 18:34, etc.

Harran A town in what is now south-east Turkey, on the River Balikh, a tributary of the River Euphrates. This was the place where Abraham's father, Terah, settled after leaving Ur, and where Jacob worked for Laban. Harran was on the main road linking Nineveh with Aleppo in Syria, and on south to the port of Tyre. It was fortified

by the Assyrians as a provincial capital. For three years after the fall of Nineveh it was Assyria's capital city. Then in 609 it fell to the Babylonians.
Genesis 11:31; 12:4–5; 29:4, etc.; 2 Kings 19:12; Ezekiel 27:33; Map p. 8

Harod The spring where Gideon chose his fighting force by watching how the men drank from the stream. The 300 who showed their alertness by stooping and lapping the water were chosen. The place was in northern Palestine, probably by a stream which flows down the Valley of Jezreel.
Judges 7:1–8

Hazor A Canaanite city in the north of Israel. King Jabin of Hazor organized an alliance against Joshua. But he was defeated, and the city was burned. Another king of Hazor was defeated by Deborah and Barak. King Solomon rebuilt and fortified Hazor, with Megiddo and Gezer. In the eighth century BC the Assyrians destroyed the city.

Archaeologists have uncovered an upper and lower city, which at its greatest may have housed as many as 40,000 people. The lower part was destroyed in the thirteenth century BC (about the time of Joshua). A city gate and wall from Solomon's time match others of the same design at Megiddo and Gezer. Hazor is mentioned in Egyptian and Babylonian texts, and in the Amarna Letters, as well as in the Bible itself.
Joshua 11; Judges 4; 1 Kings 9:15; 2 Kings 15:29; Map OT/C2

Hebron A town high in the Judean hills (3,040 ft/ 935 m above sea level). The old name for Hebron was Kiriath-arba. Abraham and his family often camped near Hebron. He bought the cave of Machpelah from the Hittites at Hebron (see *Machpelah*). Moses' twelve spies came to Hebron, and it was later given to Caleb. Hebron was a city of refuge, and one of the Levites' towns. It was David's capital before he captured Jerusalem. Absalom staged his rebellion from Hebron. Much later, after the exile, Jews returned to live there.
Genesis 13:18; 23; 35:27;

**Israel in the
Old Testament**

A   B   C   D

Abel-beth-maacah
•Tyre
•Dan

Ramah
Kedesh   Maacah

Hazor
Merom

Chinnereth   BASHAN
Sea of
GALILEE   Chinnereth   •Ashtaroth

River Kishon
△
Mt
Carmel
Plain   •Gath-hepher
of Jezreel   Mt   •Edrei
△Tabor
Shunem   •Endor   •Lo-debar   •Ramoth-gilead
Dor •   •Megiddo   •Jezreel
GILEAD
Taanach •   Mt△
Gilboa
Sharon   •Ibleam   •Beth-shan
•Dothan
Abel-meholah
Cherith Brook
Samaria   •Tirzah   •Jabesh-gilead
Plain of   •Succoth   •Mahanaim
Sharon   Shechem•   △Mt Ebal   •Penuel
△Mt
Gerizim
•Adam
Joppa   •Aphek   ISRAEL   •Shiloh   AMMON
•Timnath-serah   River Jordan
Upper/Lower   •Jazer
Beth-horon   Bethel   •Rabbah
•Ai
•Mizpah   Michmash
Gibeon•   •Gilgal
Gezer   •Sorek   Gibeah•   Geba   •Shittim
Ekron•   •Aijalon   •Anathoth   Jericho   •Heshbon
Timnah   Kiriath-jearim   Jerusalem   △
•Eshtaol   Mt Nebo
Ashdod •   •Libnah   •Bethlehem   Salt
Zorah   Sea
PHILISTIA   •Makkedah   Wilderness   (Sea of   •Ataroth
kelon•   Valley •Azekah   of Judah   the Arabah)
of Elah •Adullam   •Tekoa   •Kiriathaim
•Keilah   •Dibon
Mareshah   •Beth-zur   •Aroer
Lachish•   Hebron•
Eglon   Engedi•
Maon
Ziklag•   JUDAH   MOAB
Arad•
ar•
Beersheba•   •Ar
Hormah   •Kir-hareseth
•Ziph
Negev
Desert

10   20   30   40 Km
5   10   15   20   25 M

37:14; Numbers 13:22; Joshua 14:6–15; 2 Samuel 2:1–4; 15:9–10; Nehemiah 11:25; Map OT/B6

Heliopolis See *On*.

Hermon A mountain on the Lebanon/Syria border. It is over 9,000 ft/2,750 m high. It is also called Sirion in the Bible. It is topped with snow almost all the year round. The melting snow and ice form a major source of the River Jordan. Mt Hermon is close to Caesarea Philippi and may be the 'high mountain' where Jesus' disciples saw him in his glory.
Joshua 12:1, etc.; Psalms 42:6; 133:3; Matthew 17:1, etc.; Map NT/C1

Heshbon A town east of the River Jordan which belonged first to Moab, then to the Amorites, and then to the Israelite tribes of Reuben and Gad. It was prosperous for a while at the time of Isaiah and Jeremiah.
Numbers 21:25–30; 32:37; Isaiah 15:4; Jeremiah 48:2; Map OT/C5

Hierapolis A city in the Roman province of Asia, now in western Turkey. Paul mentions the Christians at Laodicea and Hierapolis in his letter to nearby Colossae. Over the centuries the hot-water springs at Hierapolis (modern Pamukkale) have 'petrified' to form amazing waterfalls of stone.
Colossians 4:13

Hinnom The name of a valley on the south side of Jerusalem, forming the boundary between the tribes of Judah and Benjamin. Here the kings Ahaz and Manasseh set up a shrine for the god Molech, and children were offered to him in sacrifice. It was destroyed by Josiah. Jeremiah denounced the evil of this place. Later, rubbish from the city was burned in the Valley of Hinnom. So it became a picture of hell. The word 'Gehenna', meaning 'Valley of Hinnom', became a word for 'hell'.
Joshua 15:8; 18:16; 2 Kings 23:10; 2 Chronicles 28:3; 33:6; Jeremiah 7:31; 19:2; 32:35

Horeb Another name for Mt Sinai.

Hormah The exact site of this town in southern Canaan is not certain. Because of their disobedience, the Israelites were defeated by the Canaanites at Hormah. Later it was conquered and given to the tribe of Judah.
Numbers 14:39–45; 21:3; Joshua 15:30

Ibleam A Canaanite town in the north of Israel, about 10 miles/14 km south-east of Megiddo. Here Jehu killed King Ahaziah of Judah.
Joshua 17:11–12; 2 Kings 9:27; 15:10; Map OT/B3

Iconium Present-day Konya in south-central Turkey. Paul preached at Iconium, then a city in the Roman province of Galatia, on his first missionary journey. He met with violent opposition.
Acts 13:51; 14:1–6, 19–22; 2 Timothy 3:11; Map p. 37

Idumaea The Greek name for the Old Testament Edom. By New Testament times many Idumaeans had settled west of the Jordan, in the dry country in the south of Palestine. This district was then called Idumaea. King Herod was an Idumaean. People came even from this area in the far south to see Jesus in Galilee.
Mark 3:8; Map NT/A7

Illyricum The Roman name of a land stretching along the eastern shore of the Adriatic Sea. It covered much the same area as modern Yugoslavia. The southern part was also called Dalmatia (see *Dalmatia*). When Paul wrote to the Romans, he said he had preached the gospel from Jerusalem as far west as Illyricum. There is no other mention of Paul's work in this land.
Romans 15:19; Map p. 34

Israel The land occupied by the twelve tribes. After King Solomon died and his kingdom was divided, the name Israel referred to the northern part of the land, excluding Judah and Benjamin.

Issachar The land belonging to the tribe of Issachar, south of Lake Galilee and west of the River Jordan.
Joshua 19:17–23; Map p. 13

Ituraea A name mentioned only in Luke's careful dating of the time when John the Baptist began to preach. Herod Philip was then ruler of Ituraea and Trachonitis. The Ituraeans were probably the descendants of the Old Testament people called Jetur. They were a wild tribal people in the hills west of Damascus, north of the head-waters of the River Jordan. See also *Trachonitis*.
Luke 3:1; compare 1 Chronicles 5:19; Map NT/C1

Jabbok Now the Zerqa, a river that flows into the Jordan from the east, between the Dead Sea and Lake Galilee. Jacob wrestled with an angel beside the Jabbok. Adam – the place where the Jordan was dammed, allowing the Israelites to cross into the Promised Land – stands at the confluence of the Jabbok and the Jordan. The river is also mentioned in the Bible as a boundary.
Genesis 32:22–30; Numbers 21:24; Deuteronomy 3:16; Judges 11:13; Map OT/C4

Jabesh-gilead A town on the east of the Jordan. When the wives of the Benjaminites were killed in a civil war at the time of the Judges, the town of Jabesh provided replacements. Saul answered an appeal for help when Jabesh was besieged by the Ammonites. Men from Jabesh later risked their lives to remove his body from Bethshan.
Judges 21; 1 Samuel 11; 31:11–13; Map OT/C4

Javan One of the sons of Japheth. Javan is named as the father of a group of peoples, probably including those who lived in Greece and Asia Minor in early times. The name may be connected with the Greek 'Ionia', in western Turkey, and it is used in later parts of the Old Testament for Greece or the Greeks.
Genesis 10:2; 1 Chronicles 1:5; Isaiah 66:19; Ezekiel 27:13

Jazer An Amorite town east of the River Jordan. It was captured by the Israelites and given to the tribe of Gad. Jazer was famous for its vines.
Numbers 21:32; Joshua 13:25; 1 Chronicles 26:31; Isaiah 16:8–9; Map OT/C4

Jebus An early name for Jerusalem.

Jericho A town west of the River Jordan, 820 ft/ 250 m below sea level, about 5 miles/8 km from the northern end of the Dead Sea. Jericho's fresh water spring makes it an oasis in the surrounding desert – the 'city of palm trees'. The town guarded the fords of the Jordan, across which Joshua sent his spies. It was well fortified, and the first main obstacle facing the invading Israelites. Joshua gained his first victory in the land when Jericho fell.
At the time of the Judges Ehud killed King Eglon of Moab at Jericho. At the time of Elijah and Elisha it was the home of a large group of prophets. After the return from exile, men from Jericho helped rebuild the walls of Jerusalem.
In the New Testament Jesus gave Bartimaeus his sight, and Zacchaeus became a changed man, at Jericho. The story of the Good Samaritan is set on the road from Jerusalem to Jericho.
Jericho has a very long history covering thousands of years. The first town was built here some time before 6000 BC. At the time of Abraham, Isaac and Jacob, life in Jericho was a civilized affair. In tombs from about 1600 BC, fine pottery, wooden furniture, basket-work, and boxes with inlaid decoration have been found. Some time after this Jericho was destroyed, but a small settlement remained.
Joshua 2; 6; Judges 12:13; 2 Kings 2; Nehemiah 3:2; Mark 10:46; Luke 19:1–10; 10:30; Map OT/C5

Jerusalem Capital of Israel's early kings, later of the southern kingdom of Judah, and one of the world's most famous cities. Jerusalem stands high (2,500 ft/770 m) in the Judean hills with no access by sea or river. The ground drops steeply away on all sides except the north. To the east, between Jerusalem (with its temple) and the Mount of Olives, is the Kidron Valley. The Valley of Hinnom curves around the city to the south and west. A third, central valley cuts right into the city, dividing the temple area and city of David from the 'upper', western section.
Jerusalem is probably the 'Salem' of which Melchizedek was king in

braham's day. It was certainly in existence by 1800 BC. It was a Jebusite stronghold (called Jebus) when King David captured and made it his capital. He bought the temple site and brought the Covenant box (ark) to Jerusalem. His son King Solomon built the temple for God, and from that time on Jerusalem has been the 'holy city' – for the Jews, and later for Christians and Muslims, too. Solomon added fine palaces and public buildings. Jerusalem was a political and religious centre, to which the people came for the great annual festivals.

The city declined to some extent after Solomon, when the kingdom became divided. In the reign of King Hezekiah (Isaiah's time) it was besieged by the Assyrians. The king had the Siloam tunnel built, to ensure his water supply. On several occasions powerful neighbouring kings were pacified with treasures from the city and its temple. Despite its excellent position and defences King Nebuchadnezzar's Babylonian army besieged Jerusalem in 597 BC and in 586 they captured and destroyed both the city and the temple. The people were taken into exile. Nebuchadnezzar's soldiers tore down the city walls. All the temple treasures were taken away. 'How lonely lies Jerusalem, once so full of people,' wrote the author of Lamentations. 'The Lord rejected his altar and deserted his holy Temple; he allowed the enemy to tear down its walls.' It remained in ruins for fifty years.

In 538 BC the exiles were allowed to return. Under Zerubbabel's leadership the temple was rebuilt. With Nehemiah in charge they rebuilt the city walls.

In 198 BC, as part of the Greek Empire, Jerusalem came under the control of the Syrian Seleucid kings. One of these, Antiochus IV Epiphanes, plundered and desecrated the temple. Judas Maccabaeus led a Jewish revolt and the temple was rededicated (164 BC).

For a time Jerusalem was free. Then, in the middle of the first century BC, the Romans took control. Herod the Great, made king by the Romans, repaired Jerusalem and undertook new building work, including a magnificent new temple.

It was to this temple that Jesus' mother brought him as a baby. His parents brought him again when he was twelve, to attend the annual Passover Festival. When he grew up, Jesus regularly visited Jerusalem – for many of the religious festivals, and to teach and heal. His arrest, trial, crucifixion and resurrection all took place in Jerusalem.

Jesus' followers were still in the city several weeks later, on the Day of Pentecost, when the Holy Spirit made new men of them. So the Christian church began life in Jerusalem – and from there, spread out far and wide. The Christians at Jerusalem played a leading role in the early years. The Council that met to consider the position of non-Jewish Christians was held at Jerusalem.

In AD 66 the Jews rose in revolt against the Romans. In AD 70 the Romans regained Jerusalem. They destroyed its defences – and the temple. In the fourth century – the reign of Constantine – the city became Christian, and many churches were built.

In 637 the Muslims came – and Jerusalem remained under their control for most of the time until 1948, when the modern state of Israel came into being. Jerusalem was then divided between the Jews and the Arabs – Israel and Jordan. In 1967 the Jews won control of the whole city.
Genesis 14:18; Joshua 15:63; 2 Samuel 5; 1 Kings 6; Psalms 48; 122; 125; 1 Kings 14:25–26; 2 Kings 12:18; 18:13 – 19:36; 20:20; 25; Ezra 5; Nehemiah 3 – 6; Luke 2; 19:28 – 24:49, etc.; John 2:23 – 3:21; 5; 7:10 – 10:42, etc.; Acts 2; 15; Map OT/B5

Jezreel A town in the north of Israel and the plain in which it stood, close to Mt Gilboa. Saul camped at the spring in the Valley of Jezreel before the Battle of Gilboa. King Ahab of Israel had a palace at Jezreel. It was here that the sad story of Naboth's vineyard took place. King Joram of Israel went to Jezreel to recover from his wounds. Queen Jezebel was thrown down from the palace window and died here.
1 Samuel 29:1; 1 Kings 18:45–46; 21; 2 Kings 8:29; 9:30–37; Map OT/B3

Joppa The only natural harbour on the coast of Israel south of the Bay of Acre (Haifa): modern Jaffa, close to Tel Aviv. Joppa was the port for Jerusalem, 35 miles/56 km away. The town has a long history and was mentioned about 1400 BC in the Egyptian Amarna Letters. Jonah set sail for Tarshish (Spain) from Joppa. Dorcas (Tabitha), the woman Peter restored to life, came from Joppa. Peter was there when he had his dream about the 'clean' and 'unclean' animals. He went from Joppa to the house of the Roman officer, Cornelius, and saw God at work amongst non-Jews.
2 Chronicles 2:16; Jonah 1:3; Acts 9:36–43; 10; Map OT/A4

Jordan The main river of Israel, constantly referred to in the Bible. The Jordan flows from Mt Hermon in the far north, through Lake Huleh and Lake Galilee to the Dead Sea. It is 75 miles/120 km from Lake Huleh to the Dead Sea, but the river winds about so much that it is more than twice that length.

The name 'Jordan' means 'the descender'. It flows through the deepest rift valley on earth. Lake Huleh is 230 ft/71 m above sea level. Lake Galilee is 682 ft/210 m *below* sea level, and the north end of the Dead Sea 1,290 ft/397 m below.

The northern part of the Jordan Valley is fertile; the southern end, approaching the Dead Sea, is desert, but dense jungle grows on the banks. The main tributaries of the Jordan are the Yarmuk and Jabbok rivers, both of which join it from the east. Many smaller tributaries dry up completely through the summer.

Joshua led the people of Israel across the Jordan from the east into the Promised Land near to Jericho. At the time of Absalom's rebellion, David escaped across the Jordan. Elijah and Elisha crossed the Jordan just before Elijah was taken up to heaven. Elisha told the Syrian general Naaman to wash himself in the Jordan and he would be healed. John the Baptist baptized people – including Jesus – in the Jordan.
Joshua 3; 2 Samuel 17:20–22; 2 Kings 2:6–8, 13–14; 5; Jeremiah 12:5; 49:19; Mark 1:5, 9, etc.; Map p. 17

Judah The Judean hills south of Jerusalem and the desert bordering the Dead Sea. The land belonging to the tribe of Judah. Later the name of the southern kingdom, with Jerusalem as its capital.
Joshua 15; 1 Kings 12:21, 23, etc.; Map OT/B6

Judea The Greek and Roman name for Judah. Usually it refers to the southern part of the country, with Jerusalem as capital. But it is sometimes used as a name for the whole land, including Galilee and Samaria. The 'wilderness of Judea' is the desert west of the Dead Sea.
Luke 3:1; 4:44 ('the whole country' in *Good News Bible*), etc.; Map NT/B5

Kadesh-barnea An oasis and settlement in the desert south of Beersheba. It is mentioned in the campaign of Chedorlaomer and his allies at the time of Abraham. It was near Kadesh that Hagar saw an angel. After the escape from Egypt, most of Israel's years of desert wandering were spent in the area around Kadesh. Miriam died there, and Moses brought water out of the rock. From Kadesh he sent spies into Canaan. It is later mentioned as a point on the southern boundary of Israel.
Genesis 14:7; 16:14; Numbers 20; 13; 33:36; Deuteronomy 1:19–25, 46; Joshua 10:41; 15:23 (Kedesh); Map p. 10

Kedesh A Canaanite town in Galilee conquered by Joshua and given to the tribe of Naphtali. It was the home of Barak. Kedesh was one of the first towns to fall to the Assyrians when Tiglath-pileser III invaded Israel from the north (734–732 BC).
Joshua 12:22; 19:37; Judges 4; 2 Kings 15:29; Map OT/C1

Keilah A town about

8 miles/11 km north-west of Hebron. David saved it from a Philistine attack and stayed there, escaping from Saul.
Joshua 15:44; 1 Samuel 23; Nehemiah 3:17–18; Map OT/B5

Kidron The valley which separates Jerusalem and the temple from the Mount of Olives, on the east. For most of the year the valley is dry. The Gihon Spring, whose water King Hezekiah brought inside the city walls through the Siloam tunnel, is on the west side of the Kidron Valley.

David crossed the Kidron when he left Jerusalem at the time of Absalom's rebellion. Asa, Hezekiah and Josiah, kings who reformed the nation's worship, destroyed idols in the Kidron Valley. Jesus and his disciples crossed it many times on their way to the Garden of Gethsemane.
2 Samuel 15:23; 1 Kings 15:13; 2 Chronicles 29:16; 2 Kings 23:4; John 18:1.

King's Highway The road by which Moses promised to travel peacefully through the land of Edom and the land of Sihon, king of Heshbon. Both refused his request, and so the Israelites were forced to avoid Edom and to fight and defeat Sihon. The King's Highway was probably the main route north to south along the heights east of the Jordan, between Damascus and the Gulf of Aqaba.
Numbers 20:17; 21:22; Deuteronomy 2:27;

Kir, Kir-hareseth The name of an unknown place where the Syrians were exiled.

An important fortified town in Moab.
2 Kings 16:9; Amos 1:5; 2 Kings 3; Isaiah 16:7–12; Map OT/C7

Kiriathaim A town east of the Dead Sea given to the tribe of Reuben. It was later taken by the Moabites.
Joshua 13:19; Jeremiah 48:1–25; Ezekiel 25:9; Map OT/C6

Kiriath-arba An earlier name for Hebron.

Kiriath-jearim A hill-town a few miles east of Jerusalem. It was one of the towns of the Gibeonites, who tricked Joshua into a peace treaty. The Covenant Box (ark)

was kept at Kiriath-jearim for twenty years before King David took it to Jerusalem.
Joshua 9; 1 Samuel 6:20 – 7:2; Jeremiah 26:20; Nehemiah 7:29; Map OT/B5

Kishon A small stream which flows across the plain of Megiddo (Esdraelon) and into the Mediterranean Sea just north of Mt Carmel. In the story of Barak heavy rain raised the water level so high that the surrounding ground turned to mud and bogged down Sisera's chariots, giving Israel victory. The prophet Elijah killed the prophets of Baal by the River Kishon after the contest on Mt Carmel.
Judges 4; 5:21; 1 Kings 18:40; Map OT/B2

Kittim One of the sons of Javan in the Genesis 'table of the nations', and so the name of Cyprus and of its early city of Kition (modern Larnaca).
Genesis 10:4; 1 Chronicles 1:7; Numbers 24:24; Isaiah 23:1, 12; Jeremiah 2:10; Ezekiel 27:6

Kue/Coa A region from which Solomon obtained horses. It was in the eastern part of Cilicia, in the south of modern Turkey.

Lachish An important fortified town in the low hills about 30 miles/48 km south-west of Jerusalem. Lachish has a long history. It was a military stronghold before the sixteenth century BC.

The king of Lachish joined with four other Amorite kings to fight Joshua. But Joshua won. He attacked and captured Lachish and put everyone there to death. Solomon's son, King Rehoboam, rebuilt Lachish as a defence against the Philistines and Egyptians.

The town had an outer and inner wall, 19 ft/6 m thick. These walls were strengthened with towers. So too was the gateway. A well 144 ft/44 m deep ensured a good supply of water. Lachish had a palace and store-rooms approached by a street lined with shops.

King Amaziah of Judah fled to Lachish for safety. But his enemies followed and killed him there.

When the Assyrian King Sennacherib attacked Judah he besieged Lachish, cutting Jerusalem

off from possible help from Egypt. He sent envoys from Lachish to demand Jerusalem's surrender. Lachish fell, and Sennacherib had the siege pictured on the walls of his palace at Nineveh. Archaeologists have also discovered at Lachish a mass grave from this time, holding 1,500 bodies.

The Babylonian army attacked Lachish at the time of the final siege of Jerusalem (589–586 BC). The 'Lachish Letters', written by an army officer to his superior, belong to this period. Lachish fell and the Babylonians burnt it. After the exile it was resettled, but was never again an important place.
Joshua 10; 2 Chronicles 11:5–12; 2 Kings 14:19; 18:14–21; Isaiah 36 – 37; Jeremiah 34:7; Nehemiah 11:30; Map OT/A6

Laodicea A city in the Lycus Valley of present-day western Turkey (the Roman province of Asia in New Testament times). Laodicea stood at the junction of two important main roads. It grew prosperous from trade and banking. The region produced clothes made of glossy black wool, and also medicines. Water for the town was piped from springs some distance away and arrived lukewarm. A number of these points are reflected in the letter to the church at Laodicea in the Book of Revelation. Paul's letter to the Colossians was intended for Laodicea, too, although he had not been there. The Christian group there may have been started during the time when Paul was staying at Ephesus.
Colossians 2:1; 4:13–16; Revelation 1:11; 3:14–22

Lebanon The modern country of that name and its mountain range. Lebanon in the Old Testament was famous for its forests, especially its great cedar-trees. The Bible refers also to the snows of Lebanon, and to the country's fertility. All kinds of fruit grow on the coastal plain and lower hill slopes: olives, grapes, apples, figs, apricots, dates and all kinds of green vegetables.

The great Phoenician (Canaanite) ports of Tyre, Sidon and Byblos were all on the coast of Lebanon

and grew rich exporting its products. King Solomon sent to the king of Tyre for cedar and other wood from Lebanon to build the temple and royal palace at Jerusalem.
1 Kings 5:1–11; Hosea 6:5–7; Ezra 3:7; Psalm 72:16; Isaiah 2:13; 14:8; Ezekiel 31, etc.

Libnah A fortified lowland town not far from Lachish taken by Joshua. In the reign of King Jehoram of Judah Libnah rebelled. The town survived a siege by the Assyrian King Sennacherib when plague hit his army.
Joshua 10:29–30; 2 Kings 8:22; 19:8, 35; Map OT/A

Lo-debar A place in Gilead, east of the River Jordan. Mephibosheth, Jonathan's son, lived there in exile until David brought him to his court.
2 Samuel 9; 17:27; Map OT/C3

Lud Lud, a son of Shem, gave his name to a people known later as the Lydians. They lived in the west of Asia Minor (Turkey) around Sardis.

Luz The older name of Bethel.

Lycia A small, mountainous land in the

outh-west of Asia Minor Turkey). The ports of atara and Myra, at which aul landed, were in Lycia. cts 27:5; Map p. 35

ydda A town about 10 niles/16 km inland from oppa. Peter healed a ame man, Aeneas, when isiting the first Christians ere. The place is now gain called by its Old estament name, Lod. cts 9:32–35, 38; Map JT/B5

ystra A remote city in the oman province of Galatia ot far from Konya in nodern Turkey). Paul and arnabas went on to ystra after rough eatment at Iconium, n the first missionary ourney. Paul healed a ripple at Lystra, and the eople believed him to be Iermes (messenger of the ireek gods) and Barnabas o be Zeus himself. But ews from Iconium stirred p trouble, and Paul was toned and left for dead. ome of the people ecame Christians, and aul returned to visit them n his second journey. ystra (or possibly Derbe) vas Timothy's home own. cts 14:6–20; 16:1–5; Aap p. 37

Maacah A small Aramaean state to the south-east of Mt Hermon. It is mentioned in David's campaigns and one of his warriors came from here. Joshua 12:5; 2 Samuel 10; 23:34; Map OT/C1

Macedonia A region of northern Greece whose capital was Thessalonica. The Roman province of Macedonia included Philippi and Beroea as well as Thessalonica.

Paul crossed the Aegean Sea from Troas after seeing a vision of a Macedonian man asking him to come over and help them. It was the first stage in bringing the Good News of Jesus to Europe. Three of Paul's letters (Philippians, 1 and 2 Thessalonians) are addressed to Macedonian Christians. They gave generously to his relief fund for Christians in Judea. And several of them became his regular helpers. Acts 16:8 – 17:15; 20:1–6; 2 Corinthians 8:1–5; 9:1–5, etc.; Map p. 34

Machpelah When Sarah died at Hebron, Abraham still owned no land. So he bought a plot of land with the cave of Machpelah from Ephron the Hittite. Abraham himself was later buried here, and afterwards Isaac and Rebekah, and then Jacob.

Much later, Herod the Great built a shrine round the place believed to contain the cave and the tombs, and this can still be seen. Genesis 23; 25:9; 49:30; 50:13

Mahanaim A place in Gilead, east of the River Jordan and near the River Jabbok. Jacob saw God's angels at Mahanaim, before the reunion with his brother Esau. For a short time it was the capital of Saul's son Ishbosheth (Ishbaal). It was King David's headquarters during Absalom's rebellion. One of Solomon's district officers was based at Mahanaim. Genesis 32:2; 2 Samuel 2:8–10; 17:24–29; 1 Kings 4:14; Map OT/C4

Makkedah Joshua captured this Canaanite town in the south. In a nearby cave he found the five Amorite kings who had fought against him and killed them. The town was given to the tribe of Judah. Joshua 10:10; 16; 15:41; Map OT/B5

Malta The modern name of an island in the central Mediterranean Sea, between Sicily and the north coast of Africa. Its ancient name was Melita, and Paul's ship was wrecked here during his voyage as a prisoner to Rome. All the people on board reached land safely and were received kindly by the natives. They spent the winter on Malta before sailing for Italy. Acts 28:1–10

Mamre A place near Hebron. Abraham, and later Isaac, often camped by the oak-trees at Mamre. It was here that Abraham heard that Lot had been captured. At Mamre God promised him a son, and he pleaded with God to spare Sodom. Genesis 13:18; 14:13; 18; 23:17; 35:27

Manasseh The land belonging to the tribe of Manasseh. West Manasseh was the hill-country of Samaria as far west as the Mediterranean Sea. East Manasseh was the land east of central Jordan. Joshua 13:29–31; 17:7–13; Map p. 13

Maon A town in the hills of Judah. Nabal, husband of Abigail, lived here. David stayed here twice when he was an outlaw from King Saul. Joshua 15:55; 1 Samuel 23:24–25; 25; Map OT/B6

Mareshah A town in the low hills nearly 20 miles/ 32 km south-west of Jerusalem. It was fortified by Rehoboam. Later King Asa destroyed a great army from Sudan here. The prophet Micah foretold disaster for Mareshah. Joshua 15:44; 1 Chronicles 11:8;

A grove of ancient cedars is almost all that remains of the great forests which covered the mountain slopes in Old Testament times. Cedars from Lebanon were used to build the temple in Jerusalem.

14:9–12; 20:37; Micah
1:15; Map OT/A6

Media North-west Iran.
Media came under
Assyrian control, but later
helped the Babylonians to
overthrow the Assyrians.
Then Cyrus the Persian
brought Media under his
control.

Megiddo An important
Old Testament city on
the edge of the plain of
Jezreel, guarding the main
pass through the Carmel
hills. About 20 miles/32 km
from modern Haifa. So
many battles took place
here that the New
Testament (Revelation
16:16) uses the name
symbolically for the site
of the great last battle:
'Armageddon', 'the hill
of Megiddo'.

Joshua defeated the
Canaanite king of Megiddo
when the Israelites
conquered Canaan. It was
given to the tribe of
Manasseh. They made the
Canaanites who lived at
Megiddo work for them,
but did not drive them out.
King Solomon chose
Megiddo, with Hazor and
Gezer, to be one of his
main fortified cities, with
stabling for large numbers
of horses and chariots.
King Ahaziah of Judah
died at Megiddo after
being wounded by Jehu's
men. So too did King
Josiah, attempting to stop
the advance of Pharaoh
Neco of Egypt.

Archaeologists have
discovered twenty main
levels of settlement on a
mound now 70 ft/21 m
high and covering, at the
top, an area of more than
10 acres. The earliest
settlement goes back
to before 3000 BC.
Excavation has uncovered,
among other things, a
Canaanite 'high place'; the
city's water supply system;
a fortified gateway built to
the same pattern as others
at Gezer and Hazor; a
hoard of carved ivory
objects; and a series of
stables (probably from
King Ahab's time).
Joshua 12:21; Judges
1:27–28; 5:19; 1 Kings
9:15; 2 Kings 9:27; 23:29;
Map OT/B3

Memphis The ancient
capital of Egypt, on the
River Nile not far south of
modern Cairo. The
pyramids at Giza are also
near to Memphis. The city
remained important for
many centuries, up to the
time of Alexander the

Great. Several of the Old
Testament prophets refer
to Memphis when they
condemn Israel's trust in
Egypt.
Isaiah 19:13; Jeremiah
2:16; 46:14; Ezekiel 30:13;
Map p. 9

Mesopotamia The land
between the Tigris and
Euphrates rivers. The
centre of some of the
earliest civilizations,
including the Sumerians,
Babylonians and
Assyrians, Mesopotamia
included such famous
cities as Ur, Babylon and
Nineveh. Harran and
Paddan-aram, where some
of Abraham's family
settled, are in
Mesopotamia. It was the
home of Balaam, the
prophet who was sent to
curse the Israelites, and
the country ruled by
Cushanrishathaim at the
time of the Judges.

People from
Mesopotamia were in
Jerusalem on the Day of
Pentecost and heard Peter
and the apostles speak to
them in their own
languages.
Genesis 24:10;
Deuteronomy 23:4 and
Numbers 22; Judges 3:8,
10; Acts 2:9; Map p. 7

Michmash A place about
7 miles/11 km north-east of
Jerusalem, at a village still
called Mukhmas. It was
separated from Geba by
a deep valley. But an
important route, 'the
passage of Michmash',
crossed an easy part of
the valley. The Philistines
invaded Israel and
camped in force at
Michmash, threatening
King Saul's capital at
Gibeah. Jonathan and his
armour-bearer surprised
the Philistine garrison by
climbing across from Geba
at a steep place down the
valley, and in the panic
which followed Saul
defeated the Philistines.
Michmash was on the
route by which the
Assyrians approached
Jerusalem from the north.
It was reoccupied after the
exile.
1 Samuel 13 – 14; Isaiah
10:28; Ezra 2:27;
Nehemiah 7:31; 11:31;
Map OT/B5

Midian Part of Arabia, east
of the Gulf of Aqaba.
When Moses fled for his
life from Egypt after killing
an Egyptian overseer, he
went to Midian. He married
a Midianite wife and stayed
there until God sent him

back to Egypt to help free
the Israelites. At the time
of the Judges Gideon
defeated a huge force of
camel-riding invaders from
Midian.
Genesis 25:1–6; Exodus
2:15–21; Judges 6; Map
p. 12

Miletus A sea-port on the
west coast of present-day
Turkey. Paul stayed at
Miletus on his way to
Jerusalem at the end of his
third missionary journey.
To save time, the elders
from the church at
Ephesus came to meet
him there and heard his
farewell message. At
another time Paul, writing
to Timothy, says that he
had left his helper
Trophimus at Miletus
because he was ill.
Acts 20:15–38; 2 Timothy
4:20; Map p. 35

Mitylene The most
important city and port
on the Greek island of
Lesbos, off the west coast
of Asia Minor (Turkey).
Paul stopped there
overnight on his last
voyage to Jerusalem.
Acts 20:14; Map p. 37

Mizpah/Mizpeh The name
(meaning 'watchtower') of
a number of different
places. When Jacob and
Laban made a peace
agreement they called the
place Mizpah. A Mizpah in
Gilead (perhaps the same
as Ramoth-gilead) features
in the story of Jephthah, at
the time of the Judges.

The most important
Mizpah is a town a few
miles north of Jerusalem.
The Israelites met together
here at the time of Samuel
and the Judges. The town
was on Samuel's circuit as
a Judge. And at Mizpah
he presented Saul to the
people as their king. Later,
King Asa of Judah fortified
the town. After Jerusalem
fell to the Babylonians the
governor, Gedaliah, lived
at Mizpah.
Genesis 31:44–49;
Judges 10:17; 11; 20:1;
1 Samuel 7:5–16; 10:17;
1 Kings 15:22; 2 Kings
25:23; Map OT/B5

Moab The country east of
the Dead Sea. The land is
a 3,000 ft/900 m plateau
cut by deep gorges. Moab
was the home of Ruth. The
country was often at war
with Israel, and was
denounced again and
again by the prophets.
Judges 3:12–30; Ruth 1;
2 Samuel 8:2; 2 Kings 3;
Isaiah 15, etc.; Map OT/C6

Plains of Moab The place

east of the River Jordan
opposite Jericho where the
Israelites gathered before
they crossed into Canaan.
Numbers 22:1; 35:1;
Joshua 13:32

Moreh The hill a few miles
north-west of Mt Gilboa
where the Midianites
camped before Gideon's
attack.
Judges 7:1; Map OT/B3

**Moresheth/Moresheth-
gath** The home town of
the prophet Micah,
probably near Mareshah i
the low country south-wes
of Jerusalem.
Jeremiah 26:18; Micah
1:1, 14

Moriah The mountains to
which Abraham was told t
go for the sacrifice of his
son, Isaac. The writer of
2 Chronicles says that the
site of Solomon's temple
was 'in Jerusalem, on
Mount Moriah'. (The
Samaritans claimed that
the place of Abraham's
sacrifice was not
Jerusalem, but Mt
Gerizim.)
Genesis 22:2; 2 Chronicles
3:1

Mount of Olives/Olivet
A 2,700 ft/830 m hill
overlooking Jerusalem and
its temple area from the
east, across the Kidron
Valley. In Jesus' day it was
planted with olive trees.

King David passed this
way when he fled from
Jerusalem at the time of
Absalom's rebellion. King
Solomon built an altar for
idols on the Mount of
Olives. Later, during the
exile, the prophet Ezekiel
saw the dazzling light of
God's glory leave
Jerusalem and move to
the Mount of Olives. The
prophet Zechariah foresaw
God, on the Day of
Judgement, standing on
the Mount, which would
split in two.

When Jesus rode in
triumph into Jerusalem he
came from the Mount of
Olives. Seeing the city from
the Mount, he wept over
its fate. When he stayed at
Bethany on his visits to
Jerusalem he must have
walked into the city round
the shoulder of the Mount
of Olives. The Garden of
Gethsemane, where he
prayed on the night of his
arrest, was on its lower
slopes. From the Mount of
Olives Jesus was taken up
to heaven.
2 Samuel 15:30; 2 Kings
23:13; Ezekiel 11:23;
Zechariah 14:4; Luke
19:29, 37, 41–44; 21:37;

Israel in the New Testament

A

B

C

D

Tyre

Mt Hermon

Caesarea Philippi

ITURAEA

TRACHONITIS

Ptolemais

Chorazin
Capernaum
Bethsaida
Gennesaret

reat Sea (Mediterranean)

Cana
Magdala
Lake Galilee

Sepphoris
Tiberias

2

Nazareth

GALILEE

Nain
Gadara

DECAPOLIS

Caesarea

Scythopolis

Aenon near Salim

Samaria
Gerasa

Sychar

Mt Gerizim

Antipatris

River Jordan

Joppa

SAMARIA
PEREA

1

Lydda

Jericho
2

Jerusalem
Bethany beyond
Jordan
Bethphage
Bethany

Azotus
Bethlehem

Wilderness
of Judea

JUDEA

Machaerus

Gaza
Dead Sea

6

Masada

NABATAEA

IDUMAEA

2

3

2

3

4

5

6

7

1 Judea: Roman province
2 Galilee and Perea:
kingdom of Herod Antipas
3 Tetrarchy of Philip

10 20 30 40 Km
5   10 15 20 25 M

22:39; Acts 1:12, etc.

Myra A port in Lycia, in the south-west of modern Turkey, where Paul and his party changed ships on his voyage to Rome. Myra was a regular port for the corn-fleet which carried grain to Rome from Egypt.
Acts 27:5; Map p. 37

Mysia A land in the north-west of Asia Minor (Turkey), forming part of the Roman province of Asia. Paul came to this district during his second missionary journey, but God prevented him from crossing the border from Asia into Bithynia. He passed through Mysia, travelling west, and came to Troas before it became clear where he should go next.
Acts 16:7–8

Nain A town near Nazareth in Galilee where Jesus restored a widow's son to life.
Luke 7:11; Map NT/B3

Naphtali Land belonging to the tribe of Naphtali, in Galilee.
Joshua 19:32–39;
Map p. 13

Nazareth A town in Galilee, the home of Jesus' parents, Mary and Joseph. Jesus grew up in Nazareth but made his base in Capernaum when he began his public work. His teaching in the synagogue at Nazareth made the people so angry that they tried to kill him.

Nazareth was close to a number of important trade-routes, and so in contact with the wider world. There are rock-tombs at Nazareth dating from New Testament times, and similar to the Gospels' description of the grave in which Jesus himself was buried.
Luke 1:26; Matthew 2:22–23; Luke 2:39, 51; Mark 1:9; Matthew 4:13; Luke 4:16–30; John 1:45–46, etc.; Map NT/B2

Neapolis The port for Philippi, in Macedonia (northern Greece). This was the place where Paul first set foot in Europe, in answer to a call for help from Macedonia. He later sailed from here on his last voyage to Jerusalem. The place is modern Kavalla.
Acts 16:11; 20:6

Nebo A mountain east of the north end of the Dead Sea, in Moab. Before he died, Moses climbed Mt Nebo and saw the whole of the Promised Land

spread out before him. Jebel Osha (3,640 ft/1,120 m high) has a view-point from which it is possible to see as far north as Mt Hermon, as well as the Dead Sea and the Negev. This is probably Mt Nebo.
Deuteronomy 32:48–52; 34:1–5; Map OT/C5

Negev A dry scrubland and desert area in the far south of Israel. The Negev merges with the Sinai Desert on the way to Egypt. Abraham and Isaac camped in various places in the Negev. So too did the Israelites, before they settled in Canaan.
Genesis 20:1; 24:62; Numbers 13:17; 21:1; Isaiah 30:6; Map p. 8

Nile The great river of Egypt on which the country's whole economy depended. The Nile flows from Lake Victoria in the heart of Africa, about 3,500 miles/5,632 km to the Mediterranean Sea. The fertile valley of the Nile (never more than about 12 miles/19 km wide in Upper Egypt) is flanked on either side by desert. Every year the river flooded its banks in spring, leaving behind a layer of fertile mud. Crops would grow wherever the water reached. Too high a flood meant destruction; too low a flood, starvation. The river was also a useful means of transporting goods from one part of the country to another. About 12 miles/19 km north of modern Cairo the Nile divides into a western and an eastern branch. Between them is the flat marshy land known as the Delta.

The Nile features in the dreams of Joseph's pharaoh. The pharaoh at the time of Moses' birth ordered his people to drown all Hebrew boy babies in the Nile. Moses himself was hidden in a basket in the reeds at the river's edge. The Nile also features in the sequence of plagues sent by God when the pharaoh refused to free the Israelites. It is often mentioned by the prophets.
Genesis 41:1–36; Exodus 1:22; 2:3–10; 7:17–25; 8:1–15, etc.; Isaiah 18:2, etc.; Map p. 9

Nineveh An important city in Assyria, notably in King Sennacherib's reign. The Bible says that Nineveh was founded by Nimrod the hunter. The site certainly has a very long

history, going back to about 4500 BC. From about 2300 BC the city had a temple to the goddess Ishtar.

Nineveh grew in importance from about 1250 BC, as Assyria's power increased. Several Assyrian kings had palaces there. Sennacherib undertook a great deal of rebuilding and other work.

Reliefs carved on the walls of his new palace show his victories, including the siege of Lachish in Judah. At Nineveh, too, archaeologists discovered a clay prism (the Taylor Prism) which describes how King Hezekiah was 'shut up like a bird' in Jerusalem.

Ashurbanipal, the next king but one, added to Nineveh's greatness. Whole libraries of inscribed tablets, including the *Epic of Gilgamesh* (containing a flood story) and the creation epic (*Enuma elish*), have been discovered at his palace and in the temple of Nabu. Nineveh fell to the Babylonians in 612 BC.

In the Bible, Jonah was sent to save Nineveh; Nahum prophesied against it.
Genesis 10:11; 2 Kings 19:36; Jonah 1:2; 3; Nahum 1:1; Luke 11:30; Map p. 19

Nob When David escaped from King Saul's attempts to kill him, he received help from the priest Ahimelech at Nob. But one of the king's men told Saul, and he had the priests at Nob killed. Isaiah foretold that the Assyrians would camp at Nob and advance on Jerusalem. It seems that Nob was a strong place close to the city, perhaps at Mt Scopus, north of the Mount of Olives. There was still a settlement at Nob when Nehemiah was rebuilding Jerusalem.
1 Samuel 21 – 22; Isaiah 10:32; Nehemiah 11:32; compare Matthew 12:4; Mark 2:26; Luke 6:4; Map OT/B5

Olives See *Mount of Olives*.

On An ancient city in Egypt, famous for its worship of the sun-god Rē. Joseph married the daughter of the priest of On, and they had two sons, Ephraim and

Manasseh. On is mentioned later in the prophets, once by its Greek name 'Heliopolis' (city of the sun).
Genesis 41:45, 50; 46:20 Ezekiel 30:17; compare Isaiah 19:18; Jeremiah 43:13

Ophir A country famous for its gold. It may have been in South Arabia, or East Africa (Somalia), or even India.
1 Kings 9:28, etc.

Paddan-aram The area around Harran in north Mesopotamia (not named in *Good News Bible*). Abraham sent his servant to Paddan-aram to choose a wife for Isaac from the branch of the family which had settled there. Jacob later fled from Esau to his uncle Laban, who was living at Paddan-aram.
Genesis 25:20; 28:2; Map p. 8

Pamphylia A region on the south-west coast of modern Turkey. The town of Perga, visited by Paul, was in Pamphylia. Jews from this region were in Jerusalem and heard Peter and the apostles on the Day of Pentecost.
Acts 2:10; 13:13; Map p. 35

Paphos A town in the south-west of Cyprus. Paul visited Paphos on his first missionary journey. Here he met the magician Elymas; and the governor of the island, Sergius Paulus, believed God's message.
Acts 13:4–13; Map p. 36

Paran A desert area near Kadesh-barnea, where Hagar's son Ishmael grew up. The Israelites passed through it after the exodus. From here they sent spies into Canaan.
Genesis 21:20; Numbers 10:12; 12:16; 13:1–16, etc.

Patmos An island off the west coast of modern Turkey. The place where John had the visions written down in the Book of Revelation.
Revelation 1:9

Penuel/Peniel A place near the River Jabbok, east of the Jordan, where Jacob wrestled with the angel.
Genesis 32:22–32; Map OT/C4

Perga A city of Pamphylia just inland from Antalya (Attalia) on the south coast of modern Turkey. Paul visited Perga on arrival from Cyprus on the first

missionary journey, and again when he returned to the coast.
Acts 13:13; 14:25; Map p. 36

Pergamum The first administrative capital of the Roman province of Asia (west Turkey). The first temple to be dedicated to Rome and the Emperor Augustus was built at Pergamum in 29 BC. Pergamum was also the centre of the pagan cults of Zeus, Athena, and Dionysus. There was a centre of healing connected with the temple of Asclepius (a fourth great pagan cult).

Pergamum was one of the seven churches to which the letters in the Book of Revelation are addressed. The phrase 'where Satan has his throne' may refer to emperor worship.

Revelation 1:11; 2:12–16; Map p. 35

Persia The country which conquered Media and overthrew Babylon to establish an empire which continued until the conquests of Alexander the Great.

Daniel was in Babylon when the city was taken by the army of the Medes and Persians. Cyrus, king of Persia, allowed the Jews and other exiles to return to their homelands. The Jewish girl, Esther, became queen to the Persian King Xerxes I (Ahasuerus).
Daniel 5:29–30; 6; 8:20; 10:1; Ezra 1:1–11; Esther 1, etc.; Map p. 24

Pharpar See *Abana*.

Philadelphia A city in the Roman province of Asia (modern Alashehir, in western Turkey). Philadelphia was one of the seven churches of Asia to which the letters in the Book of Revelation are addressed.
Revelation 1:11; 3:7–13

Philippi A city 8 miles/ 12 km inland from Neapolis on the coast of Macedonia (northern Greece). It was named after Philip of Macedon. Philippi was annexed by the Romans in 168 BC. It was the site of a famous battle of Antony and Octavian (Augustus) against Brutus and Cassius in 42 BC. Some years later, Octavian made Philippi a Roman colony, which gave its people the same rights and privileges as any town on Italian soil.

The apostle John saw the visions recorded in the book of Revelation when he was an exile on the island of Patmos.

Paul visited Philippi on his second missionary journey, after seeing a vision of a Macedonian man appealing to him for help. The first Christian church in Europe was established at Philippi. Paul and Silas were illegally imprisoned here but later released with an apology when they made it known that they were Roman citizens. The letter to the Philippians was written to the church at Philippi.
Acts 16:6–40; 20:6; Philippians 1:1, etc.; 1 Thessalonians 2:2; Map p. 34

Philistia The land of the Philistines, on the coast of Israel.

Phoenicia A small state on the coast of Syria, north of Israel. Its chief towns were Tyre, Sidon and Byblos.

Phoenix Paul's voyage to Rome was delayed by the wrong winds, and the ship was still only at the south coast of Crete when the summer sailing season ended. At a conference at Fair Havens the majority wanted to sail on to Phoenix (modern Finika), the safest harbour on that coast, for the winter. Paul advised them against this, but they sailed, and were caught in a violent storm and shipwrecked.
Acts 27:12

Phrygia A land in the centre of Asia Minor (modern Turkey). Most of it was in the Roman province of Asia, but Paul visited the smaller district which belonged to the province of Galatia. The main cities of this district were 'Pisidian' Antioch and Iconium. Three other Phrygian cities are mentioned by name in the New Testament: Laodicea, Colossae and Hierapolis.
Acts 16:6; 18:23; Colossians 1:1; 4:13; Revelation 3:14–22

Pisgah One of the peaks of Mt Nebo.

Pisidia A mountainous inland area off the south coast of modern Turkey. Paul passed through this remote and dangerous region on his first missionary journey, on his way from Perga to Antioch.
Acts 13:14; 14:24; Map p. 35

Pithom One of Pharaoh's two store-cities, built by Israelite slave labour. It lay east of the Nile Delta in Egypt. See also *Raamses*.
Exodus 11:1; Map p. 10

Pontus The ancient name of the Black Sea, and so of the land along its south coast. This became a Roman province, stretching along most of the northern coast of Asia Minor (Turkey). This was one of the lands to which Peter sent his first letter. The Christian message may have reached Pontus very early, as Jews from there were in Jerusalem on the Day of Pentecost.
Acts 2:9; 18:2; 1 Peter 1:1; Map p. 29

Ptolemais The Greek name of an ancient city on the coast of northern Israel; Old Testament Acco. Paul sailed here from Tyre on his last visit to Jerusalem, and spent a day with the Christians. The city is now again known by its early name Akko (Acre), but has lost much of its importance since the growth of modern Haifa near by.
Judges 1:31; Acts 21:7; (Acco); Map NT/B2

Put An African country, probably part of Libya (as in some modern Bible versions).
Genesis 10:6; Jeremiah 46:9; Ezekiel 27:10, etc.

Puteoli The port near Naples in Italy where Paul landed on his way to Rome as a prisoner. The town is now called Pozzuoli.
Acts 28:13; Map p. 37

Raamses/Rameses Egyptian city near the coast on the east side of the Nile Delta. Pharaoh Ramesses II had a palace here. Earlier this was the Hyksos pharaohs' northern capital, Avaris. Exodus records that the Israelites built the cities of Pithom and Raamses as supply centres for the king. It was from Raamses that they set out on their escape from Egypt.
Exodus 1:11; Map p. 10

Rabbah The capital city of the Ammonites (see *Ammon*), sometimes also called Rabbah-Ammon. The Israelites defeated Og, king of Bashan, whose 'iron bed' (or coffin) was preserved in Rabbah. This territory east of the Jordan was given to the tribe of Gad. But it was still occupied by the Ammonites until David's general Joab captured Rabbah. When David fled from his rebellious son Absalom he received help from Rabbah. After Solomon's death Ammon seems to have become independent again, and to have been once more a cruel enemy. The prophets denounce the wickedness of Rabbah and prophesy its destruction.

The city later took the Greek name Philadelphia, and became one of the ten cities of the Decapolis (see *Decapolis*). The name of the ancient people, the Ammonites, is preserved in the modern name, Amman. It is now the capital of Jordan.
Deuteronomy 3:11; Joshua 13:25; 2 Samuel 11:1; 12:26–31; 17:27; 1 Chronicles 20:1–3; Jeremiah 49:2; Ezekiel 21:20; 25:5; Amos 1:14; Map p. 14

Ramah A Hebrew name meaning 'height', and used of several towns on hills. Two of these are important in the Old Testament story.

One was at er-Râm, 5 miles/8 km north of Jerusalem. Near here the prophetess Deborah lived. This Ramah was later close to the border between Judah and Israel. It was captured and fortified by Baasha, king of Israel, and recaptured by Asa of Judah. Isaiah pictures the Assyrians approaching Jerusalem by way of Ramah. Later, when Jerusalem actually fell to the Babylonians, Jeremiah was set free at Ramah. The place was resettled after the exile in Babylon. Rachel's tomb was said to have been near Ramah, and Jeremiah spoke of her weeping for her children. Matthew refers to this prophecy about Ramah in his account of what happened after Jesus' birth.
Judges 4:5; 19:13; 1 Kings 15:17, 22; 2 Chronicles 16:1, 6; Jeremiah 31:15; 40:1; Isaiah 10:29; Ezra 2:26; Nehemiah 11:33; Matthew 2:18; Map OT/B5

The second Ramah was about 12 miles/19 km further north-west. It was probably the birth-place and home of the prophet Samuel, and may have been the same as New Testament Arimathea. It was also called Ramathaim-Zophim.
1 Samuel 1:1; 2:11, etc.; Map OT/B4

Ramoth-gilead A city of refuge east of the Jordan which changed hands several times in the wars between Israel and Syria. It may be the same as Mizpah in Gilead, and so the home of Jephthah at the time of the Judges. One of Solomon's twelve district governors was stationed at Ramoth. Here King Ahab of Israel was killed in battle, and Jehu was anointed king.
Joshua 20:8; Judges 11; 1 Kings 4:13; 22; 2 Kings 9:1–10; Map OT/D3

Red Sea The meaning of the Hebrew word translated Red Sea is 'sea of reeds'. In the story of the exodus it refers to the area of lakes and marshes between the head of the Gulf of Suez and the Mediterranean Sea (the Suez Canal area). It is also used for the Gulf of Suez, the Gulf of Aqaba (the northern arms of the Red Sea proper) as some modern Bible versions make plain.
Exodus 13, etc.; Numbers 33:10; Deuteronomy 1:40; Map p. 7

Rephaim The valley south west of Jerusalem where King David fought and defeated the Philistines. Also the name of one of the peoples who lived in Canaan before the Israelite conquest.
2 Samuel 5:18, etc.

Reuben Land belonging to the tribe of Reuben, east of the Dead Sea.
Joshua 13:15–23; Map p. 13

Rhegium A port on the toe of Italy, on the Strait of Messina opposite Sicily; the modern city of Reggio di Calabria. Paul's ship called here on his voyage to Rome.
Acts 28:13; Map p. 37

Riblah A town in Syria on the River Orontes. King Jehoahaz of Judah was taken prisoner at Riblah by Pharaoh Neco of Egypt. Later, King Nebuchadnezzar of Babylon had his headquarters here. And King Zedekiah, the last king of Judah, was taken to him at Riblah for sentence following rebellion.
2 Kings 23:33; 25:6–7

Rome Capital of the Roman Empire; on the River Tiber in Italy. The traditional date for the founding of Rome is 753 BC. The city spread over seven hills.

In New Testament times over a million people from all parts of the Empire lived in Rome, most of them in crowded multi-storey housing. The emperor and his government provided subsidies and public entertainments to keep the masses happy. The city attracted wealth, products – and writers and artists from all over the Empire. Great Roman roads from every part of the Empire led here. There was a busy trade in foodstuffs and in luxury goods through the nearby port of Ostia. In Rome the emperors built some of the most magnificent public buildings any city has ever possessed.

There were Jews from Rome in Jerusalem on the

Philippi, where Paul established the first church in Europe.

Day of Pentecost who heard Peter's message. Although Paul did not visit Rome until the time of his imprisonment and appeal to Caesar, there seems to have been a Christian group there quite early. Aquila and Prisca, the Christian couple whom Paul met at Corinth, had come from Rome. They had probably been forced to leave when the Emperor Claudius expelled all the Jews from his capital. The letter to the Romans names a number of Christians in Rome already known to Paul. And there were friends to meet him after his voyage from Caesarea. He was in Rome under guard for two years and during that time may have written a number of his letters to Christians in other places.

Tradition has it that Peter worked in Rome and, with Paul, was martyred here. There were certainly a great many Christians in Rome by AD 64, when the Emperor Nero began a cruel massacre. The evil and corruption of Rome are referred to in Revelation, where the city ('great Babylon') is pictured as a prostitute drunk with the blood of God's people.
Acts 2:10; 18:2; 19:21; 28:14–30; Romans 1:7, 15; 16; 2 Timothy 1:16–17; Revelation 17:5–18, etc.; Map p. 28
Salamis A commercial centre on the east coast of Cyprus. A number of Jews lived here, and when Paul visited the town he preached in synagogues.
Acts 13:5
Salem See *Jerusalem.*
Salt Sea The Old Testament name for the Dead Sea, given because the water contains very heavy deposits of salt. See *Arabah.*
Samaria Capital of the northern kingdom of Israel. The city was on the main north/south trade-route through Israel and was built on top of a hill so that it could easily be defended. The work of building the city was started about 875 BC by King Omri. It was continued by his son Ahab, who added a new palace. So much carved ivory was used to decorate the palace that it became known as the 'ivory house'. Over 500 pieces of

ivory, some covered with gold leaf, have been discovered by archaeologists in the ruins of the palace.

From the start, the people of Samaria followed pagan religions. Several Old Testament prophets condemned their idol-worship and warned that the city would be destroyed.

The Syrians attacked and besieged Samaria many times, but it was the Assyrians who finally captured the city in 722/1 BC. The people were exiled to Syria, Assyria and Babylonia. They were replaced by colonists from different parts of the Assyrian Empire. When Samaria fell, the kingdom of Israel ceased to exist. The whole area, not just the city, became known as Samaria.

By New Testament times the city of Samaria had been rebuilt by Herod the Great and renamed Sebaste (Greek for Augustus). A few half-caste Jews still remained in Samaria and claimed to worship God there, but these 'Samaritans' were despised and hated by the Jews in Judea. Jesus showed his concern for them by travelling through their land and staying with them. After Jesus' death and resurrection Philip went to Samaria to preach the gospel, and his work was followed up by Peter and John.

A small group of Samaritans still live in Nablus and Jaffa and worship on Mt Gerizim.
1 Kings 16:24, 32; Isaiah 8:4; Amos 3:8; 2 Kings 6:8 – 7:17; Luke 17:11; John 4:1–43; Acts 8:5–25; Map OT/B4
Sardis A city in the Roman province of Asia (in modern Turkey) situated at the point where two main trade-routes met. In Roman times there were thriving dyeing and woollen industries here. One of the seven letters to churches in Asia, in the Book of Revelation, was addressed to the Christians at Sardis. The church had become apathetic. They relied on the past instead of concentrating on the present – an attitude typical of the city as a whole. It had been the capital of the kingdom of

Lydia and at one time ruled by Croesus. His wealth was legendary; gold was easily obtained from a river which flowed close to the city. The first gold and silver coins were minted at Sardis.
Revelation 1:11; 3:1–6
Seir Another name for Edom.
Sela Capital of Edom. The name means 'rock' or 'cliff' and was given to this fortress-city because it was built on a rocky plateau high up in the mountains of Edom. About 300 BC the Nabataeans took Sela and carved the city of Petra (the Greek word for rock) out of the rocky valley at the foot of the original settlement.
2 Kings 14:7; Isaiah 16:1; 42:11
Seleucia (Seleucia Pieria) The port of Antioch in Syria. It was built by, and named after, the first Seleucid king. Paul and Barnabas set sail from here for Cyprus on their first missionary journey.
Acts 13:4
Senir Another name for Mt Hermon. It is also used to describe a nearby peak and sometimes the whole range of mountains.
Sepharvaim A town as yet unidentified, captured by the Assyrians. People from here were brought to Samaria after the Jews had been sent into exile.
2 Kings 17:24, 31; 18:34
Sharon The coastal plain of Israel. It extends from Joppa to Caesarea – about 50 miles/80 km – and is about 10 miles/16 km wide. Today the plain is one of the richest agricultural areas in Israel. In Bible times few people lived here. The land was used as pasture for sheep, but much of it was left in its natural state of thick scrub. The writer of the Song of Solomon (Songs) refers to the 'rose of Sharon', one of the many beautiful wild flowers which grew on the plain.
1 Chronicles 27:29; Song of Solomon (Songs) 2:1
Sheba A country in south-west Arabia, now the Yemen. Sheba became a wealthy land by trading spices, gold and jewels with the Mediterranean world. In the tenth century BC a queen of Sheba travelled over 1,000 miles/1,600 km by camel caravan to visit King Solomon and test his

wisdom. She possibly also wished to arrange a trade agreement. The remains of a great dam and a temple to the moon-god Ilumquh have been discovered at Marib, once the capital of Sheba.
Psalm 72:15; Isaiah 60:6; 1 Kings 10:1–10, 13
Shechem An ancient Canaanite town which became an important religious and political centre for the Israelites; in the hill-country of Ephraim near Mt Gerizim.

Abraham stopped at Shechem on his journey from Harran to Canaan. While he was here God told him, 'This is the country that I am going to give to your descendants.' Jacob also visited Shechem and set up camp outside the town.

When the Israelites had conquered Canaan Joshua gathered all the tribes together at Shechem. Here they renewed their promise to worship the God who had rescued them from Egypt, and to have nothing to do with foreign gods. But in the time of the Judges Canaanite worship was practised in Shechem. The inhabitants of the town gave Gideon's son Abimelech money from the temple of Baal-berith so that he could pay to have his seventy brothers killed. Abimelech made himself king of Shechem but the people soon turned against him. In revenge he destroyed the town.

After the death of King Solomon ten of the Israelite tribes rejected Solomon's son Rehoboam at Shechem. Jeroboam, the first king of the new northern kingdom, started to rebuild Shechem, and for a short time made it his capital.

Shechem survived the fall of Israel. It became the Samaritans' most important city and they built a temple here. A few Samaritans still live in Nablus, the modern town north-west of the site of Shechem.
Genesis 12:6–7; 33:18 – 35:4; 37:12–18; Joshua 24; Judges 9; 1 Kings 12; Map OT/B4
Shiloh The town where the worship tent

Ancient Rome, capital of the Empire.

(tabernacle) was set up after the conquest of Canaan. Shiloh became the centre of Israel's worship, and the tent was replaced by a more permanent building. Each year a special festival was held here. Hannah and Elkanah travelled to Shiloh to worship God. On one of these visits Hannah, praying for a son, promised that she would give him back to serve God. When Samuel was born Hannah kept her promise. She brought him back to Shiloh and he grew up in the temple, under the care of Eli the priest.

Archaeological evidence shows that Shiloh was destroyed about 1050 BC, probably by the Philistines. Jeremiah the prophet warned that the temple in Jerusalem would be destroyed just as the place of worship at Shiloh had been. But it seems that some people lived on the site of Shiloh, at least until the time of the exile.
Joshua 18:1; Judges 21:19; 1 Samuel 1 – 4; Jeremiah 7:12; 41:5; Map OT/B4

Shinar Another name for Babylonia. See *Babylon*.

Shittim A place on the plains of Moab, across the Jordan from Jericho, also known as Abel-shittim, 'field of acacias'. The Israelites camped here just before they crossed the River Jordan into Canaan. They were probably at Shittim when the king of Moab tried to persuade Balaam to curse them. Preparations were made here for the conquest of Canaan. A census was taken of men able to fight; Joshua was chosen as Moses' successor; and two men were sent to spy out Jericho.
Numbers 25:1; 22 – 24; 26; 27:12–23; Joshua 2; 3:1; Joel 3:18; Map OT/C5

Shunem A place in the Valley of Jezreel, in northern Israel, modern S'olem. The Philistines camped here before the battle on Mt Gilboa when Saul and Jonathan were killed. Elisha was the guest of a woman of Shunem, and he restored her child to life. The girl Abishag, who served David in his old age, was also a Shunnamite. The young woman called a 'Shulammite' in the Song

of Solomon (Songs) may have come from the same place.
Joshua 19:18; 1 Samuel 28:4; 1 Kings 1 – 2; 2 Kings 4:8–37; Song of Solomon (Songs) 6:13; Map OT/B3

Shur A desert area in the north-west part of the Sinai peninsula. Traders followed the 'Way of Shur' across the desert towards Egypt. Hagar fled this way after Sarah had treated her unkindly. When the Israelites had crossed the Sea of Reeds after escaping from Egypt they had to travel through this desert, and complained bitterly about the lack of water.
Genesis 16; Exodus 15:22–25

Siddim A valley (probably now submerged at the southern end of the Dead Sea) where Chedorlaomer, king of Elam, fought against the kings of the plain. During the fighting, Lot was taken prisoner, but he was rescued by Abraham.
Genesis 14

Sidon A Phoenician (Canaanite) port on the coast of modern Lebanon. Many skilled craftsmen worked in Sidon. Carved ivory, gold and silver jewellery and beautiful glassware were among its exports. Each Phoenician city was virtually self-governing.

When the Israelites conquered Canaan they failed to take Sidon. In the time of the Judges the people of Sidon attacked and harassed the Israelites. The cultures began to merge and the Israelites were accused of worshipping the gods of Sidon – Baal and Ashtoreth. Jezebel, who promoted Baal worship in Israel, was the daughter of a king of Sidon. Because Sidon was opposed to Israel and the worship of God, the Old Testament prophets predicted the town's downfall. Sidon was captured, in turn, by the Assyrians, the Babylonians and the Persians. Later it came under Greek and Roman control.

In the time of Jesus most of the inhabitants of Sidon were Greek. Many travelled to Galilee to hear him preach. Jesus also visited Sidon and the neighbouring city of Tyre. He compared Chorazin

and Bethsaida, two towns in Galilee, with Tyre and Sidon, saying how much more readily the non-Jewish cities would have responded to him. Paul stopped at Sidon on his journey to Rome and stayed with friends in the city.
Judges 1:31; 10:12, 6; 1 Kings 16:31; Isaiah 23:1–12; Ezekiel 28:20–24; Mark 7:24–31; Matthew 11:20–22; Acts 27:3, etc.; Map p. 21

Siloam A pool, originally underground, which was one of Jerusalem's main sources of water. The water in the pool came through a tunnel from the Gihon Spring outside Jerusalem. When the Assyrians threatened to besiege Jerusalem Hezekiah knew that in order to survive the city must have its own water supply, and gave orders for work on the tunnel. It is 1,750 ft/538 m long, cut through solid rock.

When Jesus healed a man who had been blind all his life he first put clay on his eyes and then told him to wash in the Pool of Siloam. The tower of Siloam which collapsed, killing eighteen people, probably stood on the slope of Mt Zion, above the pool.
2 Kings 20:20; John 9:1–12; Luke 13:4

Simeon The land given to the tribe of Simeon, in the Negev, the southernmost part of Israel. It seems that the area was considered an extension of Judah's territory.
Joshua 19:1–9; compare Joshua 15:20–32; Map p. 13

Sinai A mountain in the Sinai peninsula and the area of desert around it. Three months after leaving Egypt the Israelites reached the mountain and set up camp. Here, at Mt Sinai, God gave Moses the Ten Commandments and other laws. The exact identification of Mt Sinai is not known. It was probably one of two peaks – Gebel Musa or Ras es-Safsafeh – in the south of the peninsula.
Exodus 19 – 32 Map p. 10

Smyrna A port serving one of the main trade-routes across Asia. It is now the city of Izmir in modern Turkey. In New

Testament times it was a beautiful city with many splendid public buildings. One of them was the temple built in honour of the Emperor Tiberius, where emperor-worship was practised. One of the letters to the seven churches in the Book of Revelation is addressed to the Christians at Smyrna.
Revelation 1:11; 2:8–11

Sodom The town where Lot settled and which became notorious for its immorality. Sodom was suddenly destroyed, along with Gomorrah. Lot was warned of the impending disaster and escaped. Sodom probably now lies submerged at the southern end of the Dead Sea.
Genesis 13:8–13; 14; 19

Succoth 1. An Egyptian town. The Israelites made their first camp here on their journey out of the country.
Exodus 12:37; 13:20; Numbers 33:5–6; Map p. 10
2. A town in the Jordan Valley which became part of the territory of Gad. Jacob stayed for a while in Succoth after he and his brother Esau agreed to go their separate ways. In the time of the Judges the people of Succoth refused to provide Gideon and his army with food while he was fighting the Midianites. When Gideon was victorious he returned and punished the town officials.
Joshua 13:24, 27; Genesis 33:12–17; Judges 8:4–16; Map OT/C4

Susa Capital of the Elamite Empire until King Ashurbanipal of Assyria destroyed the city in 645 BC and exiled its inhabitants to Samaria. Under the Medes and Persians it once again became an important city. Darius I built a splendid palace here. The ruins, in modern Iran, can still be seen.

The story of Esther, the Jewish girl who became queen of Persia, took place at the royal court in Susa. It was here, too, that Nehemiah acted as royal cup-bearer. The city was later captured by Alexander the Great.
Ezra 4:9–10; Esther 1:2, etc.; Nehemiah 1:1; Map p. 24

Sychar A Samaritan town close to Jacob's well, where Jesus met and

...ked to a Samaritan
...oman who had come to
...aw water. Many people
...om Sychar believed
...esus was the Messiah
...hen they heard what the
...oman said about him.
...he exact site is unknown.
...ohn 4:1–42

...yene A place on the
...outhern border of Egypt;
...odern Aswan. Isaiah
...ctures dispersed Jews
...turning to Jerusalem
...om as far away as
...yene. Papyrus deeds
...und here record
...ctivities of Jewish settlers
...bout 450 BC (the
...ephantine Papyri).
...aiah 49:12; Ezekiel
...9:10; 30:6

...yracuse An ancient city
... Sicily, where Paul spent
...ree days on the last
...age of his voyage to
...ome after shipwreck on
...alta.
...cts 28:12; Map p. 37

...yria In the Old
...estament, Syria is the
...nd occupied by the
...ramaeans to the north
...nd north-east of Israel.
...he capital of Syria was
...amascus. In the New
...estament Syria was a
...oman province whose
...apital was Antioch on
...e Orontes.

...aanach A Canaanite city
... the edge of the Valley
... Jezreel. Barak fought
...isera near Taanach. It
...ecame one of the cities of
...e Levites.
...oshua 12:21; 21:25;
...udges 5:19; 1 Kings 4:12;
...ap OT/B3

...abor An 1800ft/550m
...teep-sided mountain
...sing from the Plain of
...ezreel. The place where
...arak gathered his army at
...e time of the Judges.
...udges 4; Psalm 89:12;
...osea 5:1; Map OT/B3

...ahpanhes An Egyptian
...own in the east part of the
...ile Delta. The prophet
...eremiah was taken to
...ahpanhes after the fall of
...erusalem and probably
...ied there.
...eremiah 43:5–10; Ezekiel
...0:18

...arshish The distant place
...or which Jonah set sail
...hen he disobeyed God's
...ommand to go to
...ineveh. A source of
...ilver, tin, iron and lead. It
...ay be Tartessus in Spain.
...Some modern Bible
...ersions translate it as
...Spain.)
...onah 1:3; Isaiah 23:6;
...eremiah 10:9; Ezekiel
...7:12

...arsus A town on the

Cilician plain 10 miles/16
km inland from the south
coast of modern Turkey.
An important university city
in New Testament times,
with a large population,
Tarsus was a meeting-
place of East and West, of
Greek and Oriental. Paul
was born at Tarsus and
was proud of it. He
returned there not long
after becoming a Christian.
But Barnabas brought him
to Antioch to help teach
the new Christians.
Acts 9:11; 21:39; 22:3;
9:30; 11:25–26;
Map p. 35

Tekoa A town in the
Judean hills about
6 miles/10 km south of
Bethlehem. A wise woman
from Tekoa pleaded with
King David to allow his son
Absalom to come back to
Jerusalem. Tekoa was also
the home of the prophet
Amos.
2 Samuel 14:2, etc.; Amos
1:1; Map OT/B5

Teman Part of Edom. The
people of Teman were
famous for their wisdom.
It was the home area of
Job's friend Eliphaz.
Jeremiah 49:7; Job 2:11

Thebes The ancient
capital city of upper Egypt,
on the River Nile about
330 miles/531 km south of
modern Cairo. Two great
temples of the God Amun
(Karnak and Luxor) mark
the site. From about
1500–1000 BC, when
Amun was the official god
of the Egyptian Empire,
wealth and treasures
poured into Thebes. But
despite the city's
remoteness it fell to the
Assyrian King
Ashurbanipal in 663 BC.
The prophets Jeremiah
and Ezekiel pronounced
judgement on Thebes (No-
Amon) and other Egyptian
cities. (Picture under
Succoth.)
Nahum 3:8–10; Jeremiah
46:25; Ezekiel 30:14–19

Thessalonica The chief
city of Macedonia
(northern Greece), on the
Egnatian Way, the main
Roman road to the East.
Thessalonica (now
Thessaloniki) is still a
major city. Paul visited
Thessalonica on his
second missionary
journey. But the anger of
the Jews forced him to
move on to Beroea. His
two letters to the
Thessalonian Christians
were written soon after he
left.
Acts 17:1–15; 20:4; 27:2;

Philippians 4:16;
1 Thessalonians 1:1;
2 Thessalonians 1:1, etc.;
2 Timothy 4:10; Map
p. 37

Thyatira A city in the
Roman province of Asia
(now Akhisar in west
Turkey). Thyatira was a
manufacturing centre for
dyeing, clothes-making,
pottery and brasswork.
Lydia, the business woman
from Thyatira who became
a Christian when she met
Paul at Philippi, was a
'dealer in purple cloth'.
One of the seven letters in
the Book of Revelation was
addressed to the church at
Thyatira.
Acts 16:14–15; Revelation
1:11; 2:18–29

Tiberias A spa town on
the west shore of Lake
Galilee. It was founded by
King Herod Antipas and
named after the Roman
Emperor Tiberius. It was
a non-Jewish town, and
there is no record that
Jesus ever went there.
Tiberias is still a sizeable
town today, unlike all the
other lakeside places
mentioned in the Gospels.
John 6:23; Map NT/C2

Tigris The second great
river of Mesopotamia. The
Tigris rises in the
mountains of eastern
Turkey and flows for more
than 1,400 miles/2,250 km,
joining the River Euphrates
40 miles/64 km from its
mouth on the Persian Gulf.
The Tigris floods in spring
and autumn. The great
Assyrian cities of Nineveh,
Calah and Assur were all
built on the banks of the
Tigris. The Bible mentions
it as one of the four rivers
of Eden.
Genesis 2:14; Daniel 10:4;
Map p. 6

Timnah A town on the
northern boundary of
Judah which fell into
Philistine hands. The
home of Samson's wife.
Judges 14; Map OT/A5

**Timnath-serah, Timnath-
heres** The town which
Joshua received as his
own. He was later buried
here. The place was in the
hill-country of Ephraim,
north-west of Jerusalem.
Joshua 19:50; 24:30;
Judges 2:9; Map OT/B4

Tirzah A town in northern
Israel, noted for its beauty.
It was one of the places
captured by Joshua. Later
it was the home of
Jeroboam I, and the first
capital of the northern
kingdom of Israel. King
Omri later moved the

centre of government to
his new city of Samaria.
The site of Tirzah is Tell
el-Far'ah about 7 miles/
11 km north-east
of Shechem (Nablus).
Joshua 12:24; 1 Kings
14 – 16; 2 Kings 15:14,
16; Songs of Solomon
(Songs) 6:4; Map OT/B4

Tishbe The place from
which Elijah, 'the Tishbite',
presumably came. It was
in Gilead, east of the
Jordan, but the actual
site is unknown.
1 Kings 17:1, etc.

Tob A region south of
Damascus. At the time of
the Judges Jephthah lived
there as an outlaw. The
people of Tob helped the
Ammonites against David.
Judges 11:3; 2 Samuel
10:6

Topheth The place in the
Valley of Hinnom where
children were sacrificed.
The shrine was destroyed
by King Josiah.
2 Kings 23:10; Jeremiah
7:31; 19:6, 11–14

Trachonitis A district
linked with Ituraea (see
Ituraea). Together they
made up the territory ruled
by Herod Philip at the time
when John the Baptist
began his preaching.
Trachonitis was a rocky
volcanic area, the haunt
of outlaws, east of Galilee
and south of Damascus.
Luke 3:1; Map NT/D2

Troas A port about
10 miles/16 km from Troy,
in what is now north-west
Turkey. Paul used the port
a number of times on his
travels. It was at Troas that
he had his vision of a
Macedonian man calling
for help, and he sailed
from there on his first
mission to Europe. On
a later visit to Troas he
restored Eutychus to life
after he had fallen from an
upstairs window while Paul
was preaching.
Acts 16:8–12; 20:5–12;
2 Corinthians 2:12;
2 Timothy 4:13; Map
p. 37

Tyre An important port
and city-state on the coast
of Lebanon. Tyre had two
harbours, one on the
mainland, the other on an
off-shore island. In about
1200 BC the Philistines
plundered Sidon, the other
important Phoenician port
20 miles/32 km or so to
the north. From that time
on Tyre became the
leading city.
Tyre's 'golden age' was
the time of David and
Solomon. King Hiram of

Tyre supplied wood and skilled men to build the temple at Jerusalem. Trade flourished. Tyre's own specialities were glassware and fine-quality purple dye made from local sea-snails.

King Ahab of Israel married the daughter of the king of Tyre. The city is often mentioned in the Psalms and by the prophets, who condemned Tyre's pride and luxury. In the ninth century BC Tyre came under pressure from the Assyrians. The city paid heavy tribute in return for a measure of freedom. In the same year as the fall of Samaria, Sargon II of Assyria captured Tyre. When Assyria lost power Tyre became free and prosperous again. For thirteen years (587–574 BC), King Nebuchadnezzar of Babylon besieged the city. In 332 BC Alexander the Great managed to take the island port by building a causeway from the mainland.

In New Testament times Jesus himself visited the area around Tyre and Sidon and spoke to the people.
2 Samuel 5:11; 1 Kings 5; 9:10–14; 16:31; Psalm 45:12; Isaiah 23; Ezekiel 26; Matthew 15:21; Luke 6:17; Acts 21:3; Map OT/B1

Ur A famous city on the River Euphrates in south Babylonia (modern Iraq); the home of Abraham's family before they moved north to Harran. The site of Ur had been occupied for several thousand years before it was finally abandoned about 300 BC. Excavations have uncovered thousands of inscribed clay tablets describing the city's history and life. The Royal Graves (about 2600 BC) contained many treasures, examples of beautiful craftsmanship: gold weapons, an inlaid mosaic gaming-board, the famous mosaic standard showing scenes of peace and war, and many other things. Ruins of a great stepped temple tower (ziggurat) still remain.
Genesis 11:28–31, etc.; Map p. 8

Uz The home country of Job, probably in the region of Edom.
Job 1:1

Zarephath/Sarepta A small town that belonged to Sidon, later to Tyre. The

prophet Elijah stayed with a widow there during a time of drought. Later he restored the widow's son to life.
1 Kings 17:8–24; Luke 4:26

Zeboiim One of a group of five early cities, of which the most famous are Sodom and Gomorrah. See *Admah, Sodom, Gomorrah.*

Zeboiim was also the name of a valley near Michmash, in the desert north-east of Jerusalem, the site of a Philistine raid in the days of Saul.
Genesis 14:2, 8; Deuteronomy 29:23; 1 Samuel 13:18

Zebulun Land belonging to the tribe of Zebulun, in Galilee.
Joshua 19:10–16; Map p. 13

Ziklag A town in the south of Judah taken by the Philistine city of Gath. King Achish of Gath gave it to David when he was an outlaw from King Saul. David recovered the captives taken by the Amalekites after they had raided the town.
Joshua 15:31; 1 Samuel 27:6, 30; Map OT/A6

Zin An area of desert near Kadesh-barnea where the Israelites camped after the exodus.
Numbers 13:21; 20:1; 27:14, etc.; Map p. 10

Zion The fortified hill which David captured from the Jebusites to make it his capital, Jerusalem. The name is often used in the Psalms and by the prophets.

Ziph A town belonging to the tribe of Judah, in the hills south-east of Hebron. David hid from Saul in the desert near Ziph, and Jonathan came to encourage him here. But the men of Ziph betrayed him to Saul, and he moved to Maon and Engedi. Later, Ziph was one of the places fortified by King Rehoboam. The site is still called Tell Zif.
Joshua 15:55; 1 Samuel 23:14–29; 2 Chronicles 11:9; Map OT/B6

Zoan/Tanis An ancient Egyptian town in the north-east of the Nile Delta. From about 1100 to 660 BC Zoan was used as the capital of Egypt.
Numbers 13:22; Isaiah 19:11, etc

Zoar One of five cities probably at the southern end of the Dea Sea. Lot

fled to Zoar at the time when Sodom and the others were destroyed.
Genesis 13:10; 14:2, 8; 19:18–30

Zobah An Aramaean kingdom defeated by David; it was between Damascus and Hamath.
2 Samuel 8:3; 10:6; 1 Kings 11:23

Zorah Samson's birthplace.
Judges 13:2; 16:31; Map OT/A5